PRAISE FOR
ARIANA REINES

"This astonishing young poet . . . is surely destined to
be one of the crucial voices of her generation."

—MICHAEL SILVERBLATT, KCRW's Bookworm

"Ariana Reines is a go-for-broke artist who honors her
traditions by being like no one else . . . Her voice—which is always
more than hers alone—is a dialectic between the very ancient
and the bleeding edge."

—BEN LERNER, *Bomb Magazine*

"Ariana Reines . . . made me realize you could be a girl
and loving and compassionate and vulgar and voracious and excessive
and ugly and smart. She gave poetry guts, and she gave me and so
many other female poets/queer poets/weirdo poets
the guts to be female/queer/weird."

—JENNY ZHANG, *Rookie*

"Ariana Reines is something special, and her book
Mercury is a shining achievement. I revere it."

—RACHEL KUSHNER,
author of *The Mars Room*

"It appears as if Reines, who adores Ashbery (their nocturnal
preoccupations and essentially religious sensibilities have much in
common), will soon become as central to American poetry today as
Ashbery . . . became during the Seventies or Eighties."

—FRANK GUAN, *n+1*

A SAND BOOK

Published by Tin House Books, Portland, Oregon

Distributed by W. W. Norton & Company

Library of Congress Cataloging-in-Publication Data

Names: Reines, Ariana, author.
Title: A sand book / Ariana Reines.
Description: First U.S. edition. | Portland, Oregon : Tin House Books, 2019.
 | Includes bibliographical references.
Identifiers: LCCN 2019005819 | ISBN 9781947793323 (hardcover)
Classification: LCC PS3618.E56455 A6 2019 | DDC 811/.6—dc23
LC record available at https://lccn.loc.gov/2019005819

First U.S. Edition 2019
Printed in the USA
Interior design by Jakob Vala

www.tinhouse.com

IMAGE CREDITS:

Page 2: Photo by Ariana Reines

Page 36: *Black Madonna of Częstochowa* (Jasna Góra Monastery, 1382, https://commons.
wikimedia.org/wiki/File:Czestochowska.jpg)

Page 52: Photo by Ariana Reines

Page 92: *Dust Storm in Liberal, Kansas* (National Archives and Records Administration,
1935, https://commons.wikimedia.org/wiki/File:Dust_Storms,_Turtle_Studio,_%22Dust_
Storm_in_Liberal,_Kansas%22_-_NARA_-_195355.tif)

Page 180: *Smile*, Liz Larner. 1996–2005, Cast Porcelain, 21 × 36 × 19 inches (53.3 × 91.4 ×
48.3 cm) © Liz Larner, Courtesy Regen Projects, Los Angeles

Page 200: *Veve for the Voodoo Loa named (Maman) Brigitte* (Chris / Chrkl, 2007, https://
commons.wikimedia.org/wiki/File:VeveBrigitte.svg)

Page 222: Photo by Ariana Reines

Page 260: Photo by Ariana Reines

Page 292: *Herm of Dionysos*, from the Workshop of Boethos of Kalchedon (*Catalogue du
musée Alaoui, 1897-1922*, original bronze with ivory inlay ca. 100-50 BCE, https://com-
mons.wikimedia.org/wiki/File:Mahdia_pilier_Leroux.jpg)

Page 330: Photo by Ariana Reines

Page 358: Photo by Ariana Reines

A SAND BOOK

ARIANA REINES

 TIN HOUSE BOOKS / Portland, Oregon

CONTENTS

GIZZARD

SAFEWAY

THE SADDEST YEAR OF MY LIFE

TIFFANY'S POEMS

NINE NEOCLASSICAL POEMS

NO MORE SAND ART, no sand book, no masters.
—Paul Celan

ARENA

DESERO

I leave
I depart
I quit

I forsake
I abandon
I give up

I let down

SON OF A JAR

There are things not found in books
Or perhaps you have been reading the wrong ones

Pulling down from a high shelf
The fabulous album only to find it

Writhing with worms. Nothing touches
Me until I permit it. Not even kindness

Can disturb my sleep. I have
Been to caves, sure. I have lived

In them. I lay on the mosses in Valhalla
But what difference would it make

To you? There are nectars hidden
In your body. Suck your own tongue.

A PARTIAL HISTORY

Long after I stopped participating

Those images pursued me

I found myself turning from them

Even in the small light before dawn

To meet the face of my own body

Still taut and strong, almost too

Strong a house for so much shame

Not mine alone but also yours

And my brother's, lots of people's

I know it was irrational, for whom I saw

Myself responsible and to whom

I wished to remain hospitable.

We had all been pursuing our own

Disintegration for so long by then

That by the time the other side

Began to raise a more coherent

Complaint against us we devolved

With such ease and swiftness it seemed

To alarm even our enemies. By then

Many of us had succumbed to quivering

Idiocy while others drew vitality from new

Careers as public scolds. Behind these

Middle-management professors were at pains

To display their faultless views lest they too

Find censure, infamy, unemployment and death

At the hands of an enraged public

Individuals in such pain and torment

And such confusion hardly anyone dared

Ask more of them than that they not shoot

And in fact many of us willed them to shoot

And some of us were the shooters

And shoot we did, and got us square

In the heart and in the face, which anyway

We had been preparing these long years

For bullets and explosions and whatever

Else. A vast unpaid army

Of self-destructors, false comrades, impotent

Brainiacs who wished to appear to be kind

Everything we did for our government

And the corporations that served it we did for free

In exchange for the privilege of watching one

Another break down. Sometimes we were the ones

Doing the breaking. We would comfort one another

Afterward, congratulating each other on the fortitude

It took to display such vulnerability. The demonstration

Of an infirmity followed by a self-justificatory recuperation

Of our own means and our own ends, in short, of ourselves

And our respect for ourselves—this amounted to the dominant

Rhetoric of the age, which some called sharing, which partook

Of modes of oratory and of polemic, of intimate

Journals and of statements from on high issued by public

Figures, whom at one time or another we all mistook ourselves for

Anyway it wasn't working. None of it was working.

Not our ostentation and not the uses we put our suffering

To, the guilt- and schadenfreude-based attention

We extracted from our *friends* and *followers*, and even the passing

Sensation of true sincerity, of actual truth, quickly emulsified

Into the great and the terrible metastasizing whole.

To the point it began to seem wisest to publish only

Within the confines of our own flesh, but our interiors

Had their biometrics too, and were functions not only

Of stardust, *the universe* as we now were prone to addressing

The godhead, but also of every mean and median of the selfsame

Vicious culture that drove us to retreat into the jail of our own bones

And the cramped confines of our swollen veins and ducts in the first place

Our skin was the same wall they talked about on the news

And our hearts were the bombs whose threat never withdrew

Images could drop from above like the pendulum in "The Pit

And the Pendulum" or killer drones to shatter the face of our lover

Into contemporaneous pasts, futures, celebrities, and other

Lovers all of whom our attention paid equally in confusion

And longing, and a fleeting sense like passing ghosts

Of a barely remarked upon catastrophe that was over

Both before and after it was too late. We were ancient

Creatures, built for love and war. Everything said so

And we could not face how abstract it was all becoming

Because it was also all the opposite of abstract, it *was*

Our flesh, our mother's bloodied forehead

On the floor of Penn Station, and wherever we hid

Our face, *amid a crowd of stars* for example as Yeats

Once put it, and for stars insert celebrities

Or astrology here, your choice, and even when

We closed our eyes, all this was all we looked at

Every day all day. It was all we could see.

We were lost in a language of images.

It was growing difficult to speak. Yet talk

Was everywhere. Some of us still sought

To dominate one another intellectually

Others physically; still others psychically or some

Of all of the above, everything seeming to congeal

Into bad versions of sports by other means

And sports by that time was the only metaphor

Left that could acceptably be applied to anything.

The images gave us no rest yet failed over

And over despite the immensity

Of their realism to describe the world as we really

Knew it, and worse, as it knew us

SILICOSIS

By the seven concentric walls of Ecbatana
And by the ravishing anguish of living with which no

Commiseration comes from the high authorities
I wish to praise the shining altar set with mangoes

In back of the nail salon
And the acts of healing and generosity being transacted there

HABOOB

I would tell   you I edited
Out what I   didn't want
To see there   but it persisted
Behind my eyes   one man
Punched   a rhinoceros-like
Man with his robot arm
A woman was having
Her makeup done   I'm so
Nervous she said   she did
Not appear nervous   she
Did not appear to feel
At all   her skull   was inside
Her face   softer and more
Loving now
Below the guts   an act
Of desperate   sorrow gets
Committed   the root
Of all sanctimony   & principled
Gestures   or an act of sobriety
Among likers   & shamers
The fear   of a green planet
Fear   of a human planet

SOLSTICE POEM

Walking toward the water
I passed a woman twerking
In an open car door
Over the lap of one
Whose hand reached out
To stroke her at the seam
Of her tight denim jean
Shorts. She held a large
Soda in one hand
The sun was setting
Over a great confusion
And a great gray grief
Which seemed to be
The acid ocean itself
Pocked with bullet holes
And sobbing in secret
At the source

ATTAR

Statesmen come to be forgotten
Even the popstar in her mitre comes to

& for that when she reaches
From where I now write you

Sediment of our relations
Now spun to so fine a mesh

Even dust cannot pass through it

LEGEND

It happened in the dire
Time

That time of the month
Men were smelling

My availability & others
Smelled it too

I'd bled on everything there was
To wear

Dilated & exuding heat
While sun motes shook the trees

& all the birds were singing
A face made of flame appeared

Inches from the face of my teacher
A light rushed toward me

& Julian in a cornfield & from the ordinary
None of it could be braided away

J made a fist
The light went out

Love it, I begged
& the light reappeared

& moved toward us more gingerly
More politely now

& abided with us the whole night
Dancing & changing its shape

Seeming to disappear into the lights
Of passing cars

& seeming to dissolve into fire
Spreading fast across the fields

.

I smelled a woman's perfume
& felt a pressure at the top of my head

As from something that wished to descend
Leave me alone, I said with my thought

I'm taking a shower now
I took the shower but all was strange

Afterward I climbed a ladder
The heaviness was still on me

& found my friend had put a beaded
Cloth beside the westernmost window of her house

Feathers & tobacco were laid on it
It depicted three peacocks

& some words in a foreign script
& at the sight of it I found myself racked

With sobs. More grief was pouring
From me than I could comprehend

& I was one
Not unaccustomed to grief

This was the sorrow of a whole people
It feels strange to declare

It was yet stranger to behold passing
Through me. "I" was not the one

In tears. "It" was.
& there began my history

Following a bird thru
The sand & its people

ARENA

Because that light was not like the others
Making us seem to be becoming a place
& because on a traffic island the sun had filled me
& because my mother was crazy
& because she was sometimes sane
& because I was in love
& then I wasn't in love anymore
& because I was hungry
& because I needed to party
& because I was grieving
& because I had studied the Dust Bowl, the architecture at Delphi,
    Judaic & Islamic legends of Moses, Midianite theology, the history
    of Haiti, Aryan horsemen of ancient Iran, the collapse of Sumerian
    agriculture, Kundalini yoga, Allan Savory's & competing theories
    on desertification reversal, ancient & contemporary methods for
    ruminant grazing, grasslands & myths of grasslands, those Hopi
    stories that can be found in books, Roman haruspicy, Hellenistic
    astrology, the life of the Marquis de Sade, one or two novels, one
    or two volumes of poetry, Bulgarian choral singing, elements of
    contemporary sculpture, certain Gnostic scriptures, my own appetite
& because you can pay a professional to cleanse you of demons with a
    chicken egg
& because the air filled first with the odor of cheap men's cologne
& then of human excrement over warming Pop-Tarts
& because one morning in Santa Monica a woman emerging from a store
Was heard to say "They don't have guns in the toy store" to which her man
Replied "I know." He was seated beside a child. "We'll get it
In another toy store" said the man. & because an ugly incense was emanating
From HOUSE OF INTUITION & because Kabir wore
A peacock feather in his cap & Krishna had one in his turban

& because King Solomon brought peacocks, TUKKIYIM
In a boat back from Tarshish
& because I fell down sobbing over a beaded cloth
& because what I had for so long failed
To see, what I had ignored, mistaking it for ornament
Was information hiding in plain sight & because there was no way to touch
What was converging on us & because once
There were oil pits near Ardericca
& a pitch spring on Zacynthus & because Iris
Was the messenger of the gods I'd forgotten & because
"The iridescence in the peacock was due to a complex photonic
Crystal" & because that crystal was silica & so
For the most part was sand & likewise the stones
To which desolate people increasingly communicated their wishes
& because glass was melted sand & Johnny Cash was attacked
By an ostrich & because pens used to be made of feathers
& because Chopin & George Sand had been miserable on Mallorca
& because there were dust storms on Mars
& sand storms in China & Israel was investing heavily
In anti-desertification efforts & because Papa Doc
Had shorn Haiti's mountains of trees & when dust from Azerbaijan
Blew into Tbilisi I lay with a nihilist in a fenced-in woods
& when strange lights appeared
At the height of the spruces there was dust on our tongues
& because I navigated by the pinecone in my skull
Same as everybody else & because a bird
Had alighted on the lectern of Bernie Sanders & Mozart
Kept a sparrow as a pet & because the mute son of Kenzaburo
Oe learned speech from records of birdsong & because
Of the bird friends of Odin & Maasaw & because the gizzards

Of fowl were iridescent & likewise the pearl
& likewise the viral "Unicorn Frappuccino" & because Big Sur
Was on fire & a hot wind was blowing over the Henry
Miller Library & because in Paradise California people burned
In their cars & because the bullets kept flying
& because the relentless spread
Of stupidity was allegorized in Flaubert's
Novels by grains of sand and because idiocy
Came down onto Baudelaire on the wind
Of a wing & because the less we could agree
The more it seemed we were revolving
Into a gem

VENICE

Tatted surfer rising from a deck chair
Sand was the place between two worlds
Waves rolling in like prayers
Like Kabbalist friends of Leonard
Cohen and I grew so aroused I thought
I might start weeping

DOWNTOWN STANDARD

The sun rose debarred
By the tall beards of the bank

Buildings   hollow beards
With windows cut in them

There must have been an agreement
Cars   roads   buggies & chickens

& eggs, the glass-fronted
Alleys deceiving sunlight into

Mirages of liquid   another
Person might say it made her feel heavy

I was willing to tarry somewhere
I wanted to do it for love

GLASGOW

Serene in the jelly of its cell
Sleep filled her ears with music

The Gurdwara was across
From the Gaelic

School on Berkeley
Street. Hello

From the Sandyford
Hotel   a wee

Seat   a bonny
Day... but it was not her

Usage to say so
Drawer of heat

On top of her pelvis
The great author remarked

Upon the beauty
Of his nurse   at the rehabilitation

Center   "but now
She won't talk to me

Look   she won't
Even look at me now"

It was said we had lost
Our appetite

For art
We wanted life now

But not "real" life
We wanted the exact science

Fiction
We were living in

We didn't want it
But had been lying so long

To appear on top
Of it and things there was now no

Way out

TENTH BODY

I was a double of this world
And though I shrank from your gaze

Stiffening, I know, visibly
When you aimed your thing at me

Let the record show
I caused my flesh to thicken to protect

What you and your connivances
And everything they presumed about who

I was and what I wanted to buy and why
Would otherwise have dispersed, translated

Moreover into money for you
And not for me, though money

Gold as it is was the least
Of what I sought. I might as well give

You the lion's share of the grain
From the land I now plow like an old

Serf. But I am no different
From anybody else. What we till

Now is spiritual, is cultural, immaterial
Partaking nevertheless of pain

Like what shimmers at my base
An obscure future even now

Exceeding all predictions
As I write you

MISTRAL

Haven't you traveled enough?
Don't you understand by now

That dust can fall on anything
In any country, on any day of the year?

That wherever you go there will be
Diseased ground your feet

Will have to stand on? Don't you see
That between the people who want

To be machines and the machines
That want to be people women

Are still, still at this late date
Running?

TO THE READER

Other credible persons saw the same light.
—John Winthrop, 1638

A couple weeks after Hurricane Sandy
I found myself on my knees sobbing

Before an image of the Black Virgin
Of Czestochowa, known in Haiti

As Erzulie Dantor. This image had been
Given to me by a gay priest I'd met

A short while before, one long
Pleasant night we spent talking & blowing

Meth, during a special period
In my life. My heart had recently cracked

Open. Fear had departed me. I felt
My middling capacities and medium

Looks beginning to become penetrated
By drops of what I had always wanted

But still, even today, cannot name.
What I am trying to tell you is I found

Myself crying sincere tears because I wanted
Someone and because I now, suddenly

(It was 2012) had a home. I seldom
Had had one, and those moments

When I want someone badly enough
To weep and to do anything under the sun

To make that person mine remain, it must
Be admitted, rare.

Can you take
Seriously one at once so arch and so

Strange, so frank and yet so withholding?
I'll wager that you can.

And/but I am trying
To escape from the problem

Of being taken seriously. And I am trying to run
Away from ugly pictures of me. And I am in flight

From the burden of my homeless mother, which
Flight is married to my desire not to overthink

How much I too extract from this ground
And from the ones who have loved me

Whose love I have failed to reciprocate
Adequately, even though I told myself I was

Lonely, and that I needed it, the affection
And the fucking, even the briefest of thoughts

If I wasn't going to disappear entirely
Like some forgotten, minor god

The thoughts that think the mind
In which they revolve are produced

By the landscape through which we move
I was pursued by pigeons and doves with rings

Around their necks. I was pursued by dead
Then living then immaterial birds

I was beset by a capacity to see life
And death as a range of colors, and that

The colors of death, purple and variegations
Of writhing humus and white and black

Like the black and white that will fill the world if you
Press gently but insistently on your eyeballs

Were simply deathly colors describing varieties
Of living and that there was in fact no such thing as death

And when I dove down below it, taking the form
Of an insect, and when I lay supine like a bug relaxing

In the sun to describe what I had seen
And how truth and falsehood were weirdly married

To the spilled milk splattered across the heavens
And in the basis of our turning cells

I also saw how though more loosely now than perhaps
Before the net that would trap me inside my life

Still hung over me, over it, over us, over me
And my naked formless life itself

As it had in the earlier years
When I bled for weeks on end, when I never slept

When I allowed vicious things to be done to me
And when I in fact wished for them and invited them

I saw how I was held by the reflection
In the screen of my computer when it was in

The off position and I saw what my phone
Saw of my face as rocks of sorrow and confusion

Were born in my cheeks to bloom and die there
Leaving serrated proof that the invisible

World was real
                    But why am I trying to talk to you now

In this of all media
Not because I have seen things no one can explain

And for which no lineage
Credentialed me

Not because I wished to pass
Out of the world and managed to

Or because I wished to pass
Back into it and was clemently received

Not because I know anything
Though I might know something

Or even because I am burning
With desire to make myself known to you

At last, in the secret place I have prepared
For us

TWELFTH NIGHT

I saw the moon waning over the bridge
The fat moon was waning over the bridge
The moon was hanging over the lighted bridge

The moon was waning over the bridge
I saw the moon waning over the bridge
I saw the moon waning over the bridge

My heart

I saw the fat moon waning over the bridge
I saw it rock back like a cradle
I saw it rock back like an empty nut shell

The moon was waning over the bridge when I saw it
What I saw when I saw it rock back like a cradle
What I saw when I saw it fall open like a cored fruit

What I saw
Clutching my black crystal claw

We went together
To Gibraltar
I saw it slanting out of me

You fell asleep with your laptop on your belly
While I was put into a car with a woman called Therese
I rode with her over the icy fields
Glassy green like the innards of a computer

If I lose my power
If I lose my power
If I lose my power
If I lose my head

Lost among the people sweating at the mouth of the port
It was my fault
I got erupted
It was my responsibility
Gray black and green garbage bags stuffed I wished with leaves

You will say
And I will say
The waving wheat
Smelled sweet
You will say what does the moon mean
Anybody can look it up
Choosing how to mean what we see
So purposefully is a strategy
It is time
I was swept away
The moon looked exactly like heartache
A fat heart gulping down its own pebbles and keys

You make me so happy
How can I write it down
Your eyelashes are like brushes

I had to line up my left eye
With a narrow arrow
A spirit easily scared away
Bleached asphalt like an unlit wick
Somewhere in the office park
I am afraid the spirits will fly out of my head
They will drool from my mouth in oil-black declamations
When the trees shake and when my hair shakes
When the sweat pools in the seam of my spine
When I decline
When I look in your eyes
Like a big boar, ice shagged in her hair
The ancient choir of fuck squirrels says Ah
The dark furred things put the fingers of their gray nimble hands upon
    the carbuncle
Upon the jewel
The apple of my eye

It was our right
We hunted at night
Our eyes shone
We bathed with our tongues

Cream fell in clots out of me
There went my health
The moon was listing to one side

When you were looking at me
It really meant something to me
Although I was in default
Crowd of pigeons murmuring
Cooing in the airshaft like doves
Chrome sky slick against the world
Etched by the fire that is willing to kill me it claims
But only slowly but only slowly but only
Every once in a while when it lets me sleep

gentle
gentle
soft
black
rubbing
rubbing
thing

gentle
gentle
soft
black
rubbing
rubbing
thing

a dip in the mouth
a water
a lint
a glass of water
a dip in the mouth
a soft pull
it is like a sigh
my sight

warm in the middle
when you put it in the middle
where you put it
we could be putting a small sleep
we could be putting a small sleep into it
a drive to a place could be put into it
we could have put a small secret into it
into the sleep stall
which is an ash wood culvert
which is a drum made of copper
which is a drum filled with oil

Horse come to charge my life
Fat tooth ripped out when you gnaw the iced rocks
Whose house is this
In the mouth of the dead cataract
The smoking chimneys at the refinery
I know they are my responsibility
Telephone towers disguised as trees
Lonesome furniture stores of Knoxville

It was like green frozen places
Snow on the motherboards
It was snowing but it was sunny
The sun through the windshield flocked
With salt and watermarks
Where the sun was moving through shadows
I met a woman called Therese
She was a Jew in the Continental style
She was melancholy, poised, and closed
Like a pearl on a bed in a box

Unbudgeted sweet endlesslessness unjealous perfection
I could smell the black earth I could put it in my hands
I could eat the apple of my eye

Twelfth Night

The dog
Lifts its leg
And pisses on the doorframe

My mistress will see you now.

I saw her once
In a strip mall
On a patio
In a slimming foundation garment
It felt colonial
It felt abandoned
She was heating a frozen dinner
Her movements exquisitely refined
A woman who had been so neglected
I was scared to gaze upon her softness
Like the gentleness of one not made
Cruel for being unloved
It was like the twisting of a dove
It was when the bird flutters at the back of your throat
It was very very sensitive

Double
Grapes
Belly split down the middle like a busted fig
No moon
No night
No night saw
Unbelievable hunger
When you had to drink the medicine raw
When a green gas curdled your guts
But at least it compelled your total surrender
Unlike love for example

In Léogâne I got hit by a truck
I can't tell you about it
It depresses the back of my tongue
And stiffens there to make me puke
The sun like raw yolk under which I tried to get off my knees
In the shaded green room from which trees were visible
Green room empty in the emperor's house
In the emperor's house where hospital work is done
In the house that is a hospital and a chapel

Raphaella said
I think to be a poet is a very beautiful thing
Because a poet wants to be right but does not want to win
And that is a very strange thing
That is a strange and beautiful thing

The blue slate receives my cheek
Like a cool mastaba on a silver pool

And I have been pressing down on my heart for so long
That it is now rectangular
A large gold bar
A brick of Algerian hash

Have you ever been a fool
I cannot describe my love
Have you ever been a fool been a fool been a fool
Have you ever ridden in a taxi
Have you ever stood and ordered a coffee
Have you ever seen a tree fall against another
Have you seen the trees shining in mediocre night
Have you ever seen a river of garbage
Have you ever seen a ravine
A ravine filled with the things of man
Have you ever seen a purple palm at the end of the day
Where the things that withhold heaven from here
Below have all been broken
I was repeating the words all the way through
They got me through
They got me through
But when I was out it was no longer possible to see their power
And anyway when I was out I forgot them
But sometimes the heavy feeling comes the sinking feeling
I have to go through again
If I could get to the grove of birches
To be like a secret bird
Semen and bouillon, my face full of pussy and chapped metallic lips
Tongue fat with use

Have you ever been a fool?
Have you ever been a fool?
Maybe I will talk to you
I cannot describe my love

A PARTIAL HISTORY
OF IRIDESCENCE

DREAM HOUSE

The pavilion has walls of rug when I'm a knight with blood
Foaming out my chainmail so I lie down on my cot in the cool
Darkness and when I close my eyes the falcons alight on my page's
Glove. I'm fine to die in there, chill seeping into my bones, cold
Spring like a Carpaccio painting.
I fold my arms to compose myself like a coffinlid
Knight, a crypto knight I mean a dreamer. I mean a man
Who doesn't exist with his rock-hard sword standing up up forever.
Since I was seventeen I've been dreaming
I'm the maid in a house, a wide house in the mountains, and I'm
A Victorian maid, a domestic, I'm asthmatic I mean
Consumptive like Chopin or Proust and I'm honest
And servile not artistic or cruel and not clumsily
Dressed. I'm ugly in the simple way of having been made
So by my servitude and not in the unsimple way of having
Pursued what I pursued as a free woman. Do you remember
The days of slavery. I do.
I am wan and dowdy and I sleep on the floor.
Once in the dream the house belonged to my father
And a man said to me in his Schweizerdeutsch accent *And Now
That You Have Entered The House Of Your Father.*
I remember the ice of a nearish glacier seeming to steam
Against the blue sky. One's eyes grow hard and gemlike
In the Alps you know, not that I am from there
Not even close. Still. In the Alps even (especially?) the dullwitted
Develop raptor eyes. My grandmother worked as the maid
To a duchess in Warsaw while her husband was gassed at Treblinka.
Then the duchess died and she my mother's
Mother had to find a new way to hide. *Hide life*
Is a phrase I've read somewhere. In a poem maybe. I keep

Wishing I were writing about tents, walls of rug,
Walls of yak felt, yurts, lying awake in my friend's mother's
Bed thinking THE TEETH IN MY HEAD THE TEETH
     IN MY HEAD
While my heart flared BIOS BIOS BIOS I though a woman could not bear
The rhythm—what it takes to sustain biological life.
I was naked except for culture like everybody else in my generation
I come from a broken home like they do and I hide it, serene
At the joystick in the command station of my so-called self
Except I try openly to hide only badly whatever it is I think is wild that I'm
Doing my best to reveal by not really hiding though hiding.
A poet can be a permanent houseguest like Jimmy Schuyler.
A woman can be homeless to escape her homeless mother.
A white woman can get away with certain things.
A woman who does not want her spare thoughts to be consumed
By lip implant rippling butt implant wet tongue in the sushi
Flatscreeny gangbangs in a suntan might for example choose
                                                        homelessness
In order to pursue with some serenity her for example let's call them
Literary researches, surveilling aristocratically only her own pathetic
Machinations, like one of the dogs
Shaped like Nazis in a guard tower in *Maus*
By Art Spiegelman while a countertenor
And a sackbut bleat WikiLeaks WikiLeaks and naked men
And men with hoods over their eyes and zappers on their peens
Quiver in citadels in which we The United States hid them. Yves Klein knew
That walls are sad: designed to immure misery
That is why he designed a house made of air. We only write
Because we're nudists but not the kind you think but not necessarily
Not that kind. Art gets

Exhausted which is why a temple, the idea of a temple, I need to go to
    a temple
Every now and again and in order to have a home
I had to play a trick on myself which is that it's a temple, this house.
In a movie from the eighties a man from California says
My body's my temple. Okay well now in my dreams of domestic
Servitude I receive small pay. I get to go across the street
And contemplate the toiletries in an Alpine 7-
Eleven. Salon Selectives, Prell, Garnier, or Pert Plus.
My hair will look like shit. I don't buy anything
I go back to the kitchen to fish out of drawers three
Iron candlesticks. The dark lady who rages over the family
Near the high vaulted hearth where I slave over a hot stove
In nothing but a dirty T-shirt like a child laborer in a National
Geographic photograph all gorgeous in the mufti of my total deprivation
The dark lady can only it seems be communicated with by me
No longer the maid, but—progress—household witch
Earning after all a salary however tiny, horse-whispering its deadest
Most psycho old bitches, sweet-talking them down from the rafters, down
Out of tantrums unthrown, unthrowable by nobody me, the inverted
V of downward-facing liberty: when you have no choice but to try to
    have chosen
What you never, never would choose. Sitting on a bench at the end of
    my exhausted
Term like a regular grownup I pictured myself shampooing my luxury
Hair in some artsy shithole, mildew streaking the torn shower curtain
Lurching across the second expanse of poverty
My ruined imagination could manage: Well I guess I could join the Israeli
Army. Why the fuck would you want to do that said
Somebody else inside my dream head. Pretty much

Dead by the time they were done needing me as their slave
I started to feel kind of American I mean like an adult sitting uncomplaining
Torso a plain physical fact over unquivering genitals,
Just meat on a stick with the vague sense that somewhere between lavish
    femininity
And state violence lay a mediocre thing called liberty.
Still, to be able to sleep at all's a procedure of waking. Everybody
Has to live somewhere being that we are here where most
Of us are not welcome. Did you know transcendental
Homelessness was a thing. But I had that dream
On a physical mattress. On an actual floor in a room with a door
That I pay and pay for. If you write you can forge
A substance that is other than the woman of substance
You are. If you do it to such a point you can find
Yourself declining substance altogether. It happens. It is a danger.
    But there will
Always be the idea of a bath or a sleep in a bed or a dream
In the head of a woman who is even beautiful visibly
Or at least groomed, or somewhat fresh
Or like that most domestic of bugs the cockroach
Dragging his ponderous suit of armor across the floor
Or clean sheets when it's raining and I love you so much
And I think Gimme Shelter, which is a movie I've never seen

WITHOUT A WORD

Constant hissing

Redness in my upper

Abdomen & even my right

Hand is swollen with unspent

Descriptions

All night the silence

Roared in my ears & sour

Liquid poured into my joints

Every possible way to write

What's happened closing

In

SANDRA

I'm sitting in a mercy
The small mercy of an apartment I can't afford
Where the cock down the street
Still crows all afternoon & into the evening

I've been away for months
Fighting my part of the war
And because I could not desert my post
My tongue has dried out
And no part of my word would cohere
But put that in the future tense
Nothing will cohere or gel until I find out how to speak again
Until I find out whether I can.
          .

I don't know how
& something very large in me does not
Want to know how
To say the right thing
To say anything at all
It just wants sobbing
It wants the true feeling
It wants the fall
          .

I need to vomit
          .

I don't want to go past it
          .

Stay with the vomit
The word sad is like a tinker toy that is stuck in my gullet which does
not prevent me from walking or speaking but merely embitters my soul
for all time
.

Something lurches away
The planet tilts
I worry about the other side of the camera
The other side of seeing being
It doesn't stop them
It doesn't stop them
It doesn't stop them at all
An act of naked rapacity committed before the eye of god
in the fourth century
Is recorded in its consequences
Generation after generation
In the lunges & lapses something Satanic
Still sucking at the marrow of life
& venereal with lust to leave no soul alive on Earth
We now have the particulars
Every cell of loathing
Since there is more & more on film & as black blood soaks the sore wad
Of cotton stuffed high into me & my head
& world congeal in TV snow
I am swollen & angry
It is unsayable
Because the saying feels futile
& because enough cannot be said
& it is no longer a matter of words

NOT THE BIRDS

Of irreversibility

& despite pride in the act, remorse

Birds are singing & buds

Show on both bare

Tress out my window

Beads of rain clinging to the underlip

Of the wrought-iron bars through

Which I see the neighbors' green

Bars, their roof painted pearly

Insulating white, the old

Milk in the sky

It's December 23

Nobody knows what time it is

Not the birds

Not me

I AVERTED MY EYES FROM THE ROCK

Harry Partch in my ears

Not hiding the filth

Steaming lightly falsely

Impetuously out of this ground

She said it wouldn't happen

She was wrong

Birds all screaming

Man with etched fine mouth opposite me

Reading an elegant old paperback

Bearing the single word FILM

I averted my eyes from the rock

Star on the subway in the middle

Of the rain. She looked up

From her notebook and stared

At me, *devoured*

Me as they say, *with her eyes*

Then bent back down over

The page, set upon it

Like something hungry

And long-starved

She recognized me and with great

Disappointment, I felt, for

I knew I was quote

Unquote staying alive

And on my way in

On my way to staying in

Bound for the wrong

Lover's house

MAGAZINE FEMINISM

I could not be said to have "wound
Up" anywhere but it was true

That at that time I was alone. Also
True was that I had not been fucked correctly

In what was starting to feel like a long
Time. I used the apps but did not

Show myself on them to be a person
Sipping cocktails on an inflatable dolphin

Nor was I a person about to simply say
Who she was and what she sought. I got

More attention, of course, than I could possibly
Return, and at a rate of about one in a thousand

Encountered someone with whom I felt
What is commonly termed "a spark."

My appetite for self-advertisement having
Become, admittedly, low since the period

I had to take the university to court and the time
Before that when I was being stalked by several

Men and the ex-wife of an ex-boyfriend.
I was certainly having a profound experience

Of myself and of the light that fell on me
And my views, and the distortions of my views

And the cheaper versions of things I had done
Which shone in the light my machines gave

I just don't even have words for what it felt like
I don't have words for when you would rather work

Than fuck but to borrow a phrase
From an old jazz song it can happen to you

I am tired of the ruse of emptiness that fills
My sexual imagination when I feel beauty

Of a certain kind being done to me
And tired also of the job of performing

Sovereignty according to these old rules
Some of my favorite people seem to be fueled

By pure rancor. By rancor alone.
I can't say I'm the same

The sun warms my writing hand
I forget all the time

That the sun is our friend
I often forget that I have friends

I taught myself to surrender
It was strategic, like going out

Of your body while somebody fucks you
And you don't want it

Every woman knows what this is like
I don't know a single one who hasn't done it

But I taught myself another kind of surrender too
I did it in the off hours, in whatever time and space

I could steal from my career. All I can say is
Once you have surrendered like that

It becomes hard to care about magazine feminism
Though I find myself looking back at it

Like the doomed woman from the myth
And looking back at everything else too

My barbaric homeland, I beheld it from deep within a jewel
I looked down at it from airplanes

I studied it with unkindness
The way I had learned to study my own face and body

The bad ideologies through which we all
Had to move could be shaken off, and our mutual

Dependence on the machines to fill the desert
In our lives with music and bodies, ideas and fun

I would not change it for a mountain
But so many mountains had already fallen

And it may be that my despair that day
In a light of pale beaten

Gold, like something in an Attic
Vision, while an eclipse progressed

That could not be seen, it may be
That my despair was chemical or that

It was menstrual, but it was also
Mensual, actual, or it was all a bad dream

I too a product of magazines
And yet, I wanted to say, and yet

Some wild feature of my apparent docility
Is even now filling my arms

As if it were a cayenne pepper soda
I were talking to you through

But now I feel the other world pulling me down
Again... Goodbye

I CAN'T GIVE YOU ANYTHING BUT LOVE

The sun was setting between two pillars of Michaels

Both red within like me

Whose blood refused to shine

Today & these thirteen nearly

Thirteen days now I've lived

Without love

When M called it turned out we had both

Been reading Baldwin. He told me

About the time he and Susan

Sontag became lovers in New Mexico

She had booked a room for them to get

Massages. Truth or Consequences.

Both were naked

She wanted to show

Him her mastectomy scars

"And you know me," said M

"I licked them."

The sun was acid bright on the wrought-

Iron edges and on all the buildings

With shadow the color of powdered

Bone & purple lips of ocean things

My ovaries like two andirons

Acid Maxfield Parrish light

In which the gold of the water

In the pores of the fingers sparkled

& the grooves of fingerprints were

As jacquard

An insolent unsanitary light

Whose sun falls on us

At the winter angle

Whoever we are

BOHEMIAN RHAPSODY

The past was a thing

A sucker to melt in the mouth

History

A brand

Hovering over the event

A person the moist place

Into which a thing, invaginated

Dissolved

Into poison

Into food

Into "waste"

My stranger

Whose face

I'll recognize long

Long after I'm gone from here

This sucker is ancient

Still in its wrapper

Dried Diane

Arbus candy

A feeling like "history"

O America

O Twentieth Century

I can still taste you

I can taste your waste

In my own unspent

Potential

I would

Have tweeted these things

But my computer was broken

So down it went

Out my white pen

Down the vein

Of my right arm

Beneath which my

Innateness vibrates on the seat

Of the train

Change in pockets

Cleanest of all mornings

To awaken from such

Antiquated dreams

"Global warming" they said

But it was called Climate Change now

Morning of unutterable

Brilliancy

Light pomaded with all

The false summers

Of all the cosmetics

In all the Sephoras

But beautiful

(But beautiful she said)

And like the blonde Palestinian

Stripper whose voice

With that early-twenties too-

Loudness of the wounded

And assertive and tender

Revealed something

Of the permanence

Of her promise

To her own dissatisfaction

(Praise, praise her rage)

O Baldwin

The beauty of your characters'

Commitment to loving

In their own way

No matter how difficultly

Their own ways unfurl

No matter how lonelily

They never suffer without

Your compassion and so

The world suffers with ours

RAMAYANA

for Carina Finn

Here is where I first stood transparent

To my mind. You must have seen me

But I can't tell you when it began

When my friend was opening her bluefish

Laying lemons all along his chilled raspberry

Flesh. Not then. But here

Like a foretaste of dental rot

I nearly caught an eel once

He tied himself in knots

Frightening away all the fish

The penny in my little pussy convulsed in horror

When I know

What I know

That's not a shadow in your kitchen

It is a bug shimmering

Look at him waving his rays

Inside you tickling all you don't

Want to know that you know

This shoe I drag survivalistically

Beneath the tarted perambulator

In which by God I have seated my soul

To get fucked by this shoe

By the mistress whose walk is a shoe-limping fuck

By the mistress whose limp is a bone-fucking bed

Whose past is a braid

Whose first is a maid

Whose last are tongues

Of flame, strawberry slabs

Salivating up the ass of the bear

I crown myself with this diadem

Spunk and wool

Osso buco

You are alive in Torino

There I go kneeling

Supplicant to the years here I go

Knighting myself in my tits

In zits like iron ball bearings

In ball-and-chains ballasting

Us to the beginning

Of the end of this world

SOMETHING INSIDE ME

I want to lie down on my belly
Be seen by nobody
When I extend my heart across this city
Not to feel for it ever again the way I used to
There was a sensation in me I thought I'd gotten rid of
Now it is back again and bigger
It is here
I open a beer

Out of the cradle endlessly rocking
The moon rose laughing and ochre
I gave the boy at the Duane Reade register my number
He handed me the costly thing I'd put down on the counter
I'd lost the nerve to shoplift it but then he started showing me his tattoos
You forgot something he said the manager by his side amused
So I acted happy; cocky. Threw the thing in my bag. Sauntered out
    trying to teach myself
A lesson: You brood on wounds Ariana but they are not it. What it is is
    the light they emit

A blonde woman kissed me hard outside the party
I was so depressed and ugly. It was time to nullify my identity
You're sexy she said who are you
I'm lost I thought as I ran down the stairs
There is this strange insistence in brilliant women that is so differently
    sexual but anyway
I am illegible asshole is what I'd like my eye to say and sometimes it does
When it speaks its impossible sorrow to the world it sees
I want to be hidden like the scroll in the ark and come out only on God's day

Not true. But I want to hide like a gold statue in the belly of the holy of
    holies
Or else I risk mirroring you
I do. I really really do. And it hurts that I can't tell the difference
When you stick your finger in me just to see if I'm there
When I tell you you can put your finger in me if it will make you believe
    that you're there
Like the deaf boy I met last night on Bogart Street. I'm deaf
He said and held out his BlackBerry. What's your name he typed.
He was wearing prayer beads. We can't help but love what gives us life,
    even bad life

I guess. Like love the street I mean. My heart melted. My heart is
    rubber and blind
From everything I've seen through the glasses on my head
In front of my eyes that touch the world that can be seen
When I look at a painting on my laptop that shines back at me
When I drag my little brother through the Egyptian Wing
You should project your body into ancient times Michel advised
I already do I said. And the idea of Europe devolves into a Teutonic
    moment in Brooklyn
In which we got to be Jews in a beer garden and got shitfaced and it was
    others who died

Not us. It is the look of love that still scalds
My heart which is why the visible world reflected in art
Even though I shit on art is the only truth
Whatever lives inside me can bear of the visible world some days.
    Today. Something
Inside me that can and did love a wrecking ball

And quiver in harmony with the planet wobbling
Upon its axis. To paint is manual
As Thomas might have known had he painted. To conflate the eye with
    the hand

A lot's changed in the way I regard
You and that scares the shit out of me I almost wrote
Someone just now. The sun is seen in parts of the flotilla and glances
Off my horns. The air is wet with heat. Where I end
And you begin is your problem not mine as soon as I set
This down. The hand goes dark
All the way up the genital ripped through my belly
My back against the building last night in a neighborhood I never knew
    as an actual one

Which is already unrecognizable. Hélas the human heart with respect to
    the city blah blah blah
But I never even loved this place. Did I. Well I knew it. To know. To
    love. I'll stay
A little longer. Because last night I had a sweet feeling in an uncherished
Place. What if I learned to cherish what is before me for the simple reason
That it is truly before me. To love like that. Us; here. Didn't I decide
    in these times
I am not allowed to die artistic deaths. Even though all my loves come
    here to die.
Even though I do not doubt that the stasis of action that walks down
    the street
Here is a timeless errancy that is also an error. It could be nineteen fifty

Or twenty fifty in the street when we walk down it I mean like we are the foam of the cream
Of the world passing through here to be seen and touched. To be persons, a haze, an aura
Of gazes full of temples, palaces, and hovels. Suppose it were for each other we came here
With mystical ears and subtle hearts in a dismal smear of something so human it's nude
And shines lustrous and killing in the eye and believes it won't die
For what it merely *is* but is willing to die *for what it loves*. And live by it. I mean us
In attitudes of competition and self-composure and nobility and collapse
Naked and willing to try. I could love differently. I could

A VALEDICTION FORBIDDING MOURNING

after the rain hit
the creosote the sun
hit it & a fragrance
wild & sweet was hitting
me, a springtime
sensation of rising seed
confusing the seasons
undoing the doom i clasp
& unclasp like the warm
gem in the keats poem
but this was not the prescription
you asked for
& the moon is full
not new. i came to truth or
consequences for my
own safety. i had passed
thru the doors of bellevue
under the sign "EMPLOYES" [*sic*]
to face my parent
in donated shoes, without
her wig, clothed in hospital-
issue pajamas & all her illusions
scummy, like an old fish
cooked to death
a rubber gag version
of a human aura, i'd passed
thru a nite out w eileen
jill masha
& emily who when
eileen introduced

me said, "the playwright?"
it never occurred to me
to think i might
be one of those. *telephone*
changed my life said emily
it changed mine
too i said. but a narrow
alley of reportage dividing
my predictions from
this report should keep
me in my lane.
                    did you see
the moon this morning
asked a man in passion
pie cafe. by god
it was beautiful, it was
huge & so bright he
said. at the new
moon i was in buenos aires
bleeding, with a kavanaugh
migraine, a little bit falling
in love w everyone
savoring the terror
& the motes
of death in unfamiliar angles
of the sun which felt like history
to me, the tortured
& disappeared parents
of my new friends, a burnt
andean redness   the avenues

awash in it   pyramidal mandarins
& walls of cilantro & cabbage
acreages, the pampas for real
lush with mud & cattle
a sow with eight rows of full-on
breasts & kavanaugh just
kept bleeding, now into
the effluent of dictatorship
churning thru the ducts
in the hearts of the artists
sweating on the dancefloor
kissing three at a time
into the demagogue rising
in brazil. sorry ceci
said we are preoccupied
with the news. so am i
i said, we all are, even if
it's true when you're away
from your own country
the quarrels in another
seem "understandable"
in the way no response
to anything cannot somehow
be construed as human
& even if profoundly unjust
somehow part & parcel
of the greater, deeper, more horrible
& boundlessly sweeter justice
of the unfathomable whole
but my friends

were all so new & so very
beautiful, pounding
their beers & huffing
their bumps & eating
their cigarettes
determined to go on
all night, forever
making & talking
fucking thru the changing
of the guard, the supposed
obsolescing of jazz

venus turned backward
in sympathy with lot's wife
& does a slow & mournful quadrille
thru the moshpit
dust in her eye
spit, mud & cum on her dress
as though wading through a world
that had forgot it's
sweetness that makes life
worth living, that makes you
want to live
& sweet alreadiness
a kind of rare trust
when you behold
a hand that shows
it knows the weight
of every last thing
it has ever ever held

a bovine truth
old-fashioned
beauty. i mean the kind
you can see & touch
the kind that means
the ground, unraped
pushes up the seed
acclaims your foot
admits your body
before & after
your departure
& blowing up the symbols
of the old left
which almost but didn't
happen today
seems part of the exploding
ground of reality
itself, where the true
revolution is in the soil
not in the righteous
indignancy of victims
which the very worst
among us also believe
ourselves to be

a strategy of the freedom
riders, a thoughtform
under which they trained
was to receive blows
as though they'd volunteered

for them. this might be the last
& only way to short
circuit the bad that may
converge on you. the truck
driving into you. the police
the heavy body holding
you down & sliding
into you to bury
its poison in you for as long
as you'll be the fertile
ground for the blooms
the dealer thought
better to discharge in you than
transmute himself some other
where, who had no art
to tell his badness
to or if he did
it was a false art. when the very
worst emerges, the blue
wave not rising quite high
enough to clear the seawall
think hard on when last you
were the one slamming
the poison into yourself
and of your own volition

we repeat what we undergo
until a grace arrives
if i am compelled
i will refuse
if my refusal is met with blows
i then reject compulsion
and volunteer my neck to the knife
i demand grace
i insist on grace
i volunteer
this is what the saints did
not endure but transmute
the bad done to them
into a coin, redeemable
in the cosmic economy
like the rat offering her
brains to our science
and like the cow
whose flanks i sink
my teeth into
sacrificial taurean
meeting her end if not
in outrage then, in a curving
grandin on-ramp,
quietly and beautifully
secreting none of the ointments
of horror that damage
the products of her death
& locking the moon & sun
in our horns, onward into
the thinning of the veil

you must
you must stop lying to yourself
you must drop the rationalizing
or else mercury will stop
being your friend. he has every
right to fuck with you.
saturn would steady, not scold
you if you could learn to stop
flinching when under his eye
& as for the pornographic
suffering manufactured
for us by the television
writers, that suffering
& the serial elaboration
of endurance that seems to make
us feel better about our own
lot, when uranus dips
back into the sign of the self
he will need a lot of space
figuring out how to make
enough room to be in you
is how the bardic gift
descends the spinal column
reaching down into time
past & time future, digging
down to china, li po
drunk & witnessing himself
in the light moving like a hand
over the mountains.

on my last night in buenos
aires juliana kept saying
you don't look american
you know how to talk with your eyes
maybe it's cos i don't
speak the language
no, no said juliana
who is despotically
kind, that is not why
i could tell you more
but to the extent
i can be truthful
while speaking generally
& the extent
to which i can be personal
while writing publicly
more will not be wise
sweetness has a shelf life
you don't have to give yourself
to everyone you want
just like every impulse
need not be surrendered
to. whose mind is this
anyway? beholding
my mother in the visiting
room i felt i was sitting
with a shamed & ruined
god. if you were god
how would you treat
yourself? imagine a god

losing all her power.
how would she get it back?
or maybe discover
a different power
altogether, just lying there
among the rejects
in the filth
upon which the egalitarian
sun falls
urging you to come to life

GIZZARD

Dust Storm 4-14-35
Turtle Studio, Liberal, Kans.

Go, go, go, said the bird
—T. S. Eliot

11/22

A bullet's like a planet
Orbiting the brain
No heart will go unpunished
Tho it never enter in

For tho it didn't enter
Yet it did & does & shall
For tho we only saw it
It is moving thru us still

MECUM MEA SUNT CUNCTA

There was no way to put my arms

Around it, but it was moving

Through me all the way down, into

The dark. I learned how to say

Thank You in the language

Closed my heavy bag & saw

The sun rise. The same songs

Were playing there

Green figs went rose then

Luscious to rot. Parody

Of feeling circulated

"Freely" wherever you went

Magnificently painted woman

Under her black cloth, leading

Her child by the hand. Men

In white caftans leading their

Wives. The beauty of money

Shining in a young

Eye. The beauty of reciprocating

Gazes. The rare gentleness

Of a woman's eye upon herself

What does money mean in heaven?

Jupiter raping Danaë as a shower

Of gold. I live by the force

Of invention. It and you

"Literally" everything I have

CONTENDER

He told me it was a game...
That it was a game when all the pigeons
Were circling... He told me it was a game
Between rival buildings and that they all
Keep pigeons and that sometimes they
Compete... He told me when you see
A flock of pigeons swirling in Queens look
Around you'll see another flock swirling
And that it's a game. He was a handsome
Man on Myrtle Avenue. They're pretty huh
He said. I started smiling. You want one
He asked. I want one I said...

ANOTHER DREAM

Tea bag bloating like a body
The tea would now slide down her throat
In an atmosphere of cockroaches
& white alligators & the withdrawal
Of money & sex, tawny like the two
Bobbins toward the left of her guts
Which turn to tighten the last of her
The last of the substance that generates
Soul-stuff without which she cannot live

In Greece now. Rocks
Upon the shore in the form of arches
Partway into the crimson water
Walking along the strand
In Naxos, "the great, relaxed curve
Of time" easing toward a strange
Open square of white marble.
"The ruin."

There was something Californian
About this kind of money, like
A strand of fish excrement snaking
Thru the palms
Coming through this opal
Night to her
To her without her pills

IT WOULD BE A SMOOTHNESS A JESUS

It would be a smoothness, a Jesus
Smoothness to come languishing now
To look languishingly at her
A rough woman from a century
Of rough women whose assent
Was won violently, won at great
Length by the state, their husband
Down to the very last one of them
Who dared, like a nymph refusing
To marry, to try and turn herself
Into a tree

MAINTAINING INTACTNESS OF THE SILLY

Small cellulite of the upper arms
Maintaining intactness of the silly
Putty genital I'd rather eat
Than fuck I'd rather read than quote
Unquote make love, yearning to turn
From symmetry my eye wants
To goggle. I was looking at his sleeping
Countenance, as steadfast as one dead
The moon was rotting

THE END OF ME

It's been months since I squeezed
White pus from a zit but last night
After falling asleep with J in front
Of the Bukowski documentary
I did it to two. Was I still
Bleeding? Decided not to replace
The loaded tampon, removed
For sex & drying like a dead animal
Beside the bed. My sheer red
Panties were on the small side &
Rather chafey. J's been working
Out. Really? Long arms the color
Of almond paste & hard. Belly
Of an unaccustomed hardness.
He gets results I guess. I need
To shit then drink a glass
Of nettle tea & clean the cat
Box. New York's gonna be
The end of me

I HAD AN IDEA OF SYMMETRY

I had an idea of symmetry

Bordering on theology

That dictated I consume

Darkness in proportion

To "the world's"

The many philosophies

Celebrating equanimity

Kindness and happiness

Propagated by saints

And sages from Tibet

And Vietnam and other

Places felt as yet

Incommensurate

To my rage

And triteness

My unslakable sorrow

And the narrow

Idea of victory

I apparently shared

(My struggles aside)

With even the worst

Men of my culture

But in a way I had

To become an idiot

At least partially

In order for what

Happened to me

(I will relate it)

To happen or

So I tell myself

English connives

I mean contrives many

Routes to the unseen

But turns out to be

An awkward conveyor

I keep thinking I won't

Have been able to

Describe what I've yet

To set down in a place

You might find it

But I did describe it

Description's old-

Fashioned. I know it.

But in this case there

Was no other way

BOOMERS

They taught us the world
Was ending but they were wrong

They hardly taught us anything
Hiding themselves

In the cantaloupe
Light at the witching

Hour
Our parents, badly

Harmed, desperate
But unkind

Clinging
To whatever

They could remember
From the war

And to the phrase
Before the War

Which they carried
Into the next

Country
With a couple of coins

A stick
Of furniture

Hairs sprouting
From their tough old leg

He understood there
To be feeling

In it
But he did not

Know
What feeling was

The heart has brain
Cells in it

My lover said
Since before

I reached
Majority

My country has been at war
My adulthood entered war

In parallel to the decline of her art
Which could not be protested

Only soaped like gray water down
The flocked back of a stone

Maiden
Hypnosis of scents & of forms

Gag teeth
Make no sound

Poker chips
Chips you can't eat

I'll put my money on the crystal
Children

Your own career
From LAX to El

Pollo Loco like all
Truly natural

Things at last
Completed

In the dark
And in silence

Unacclaimed

THE REAL WAY THINGS NEED TO GO

You'll need to clear your schedule if you want to see this
I'm going to be made a mockery of and I'm going
To be misunderstood within myself, the show
Is about to start, ok now. NOW. I'm doing it
Now, Great Beauty, whipping
Me with your little wing, with your famous
Little wing. You play about the edges of the wound
Castigating us for our lack of faith, LACK OF FAITH
You keep saying IS WORSE THAN WANT
OF DISCIPLINE. He kept his room clean.
He was kind of the most beautiful man I had
Ever seen. When you turn away the evening bevels out
The sides of your face. The wind massages your worser
Scars. And now the banker has released your funds.
A tower of people goes up in flames. Was desire just
Another way of doing violence to another without
Appearing to? The real way things need to go
Was averse to a lie I had to tell, dirty laundry
Dangling over the heart of the city

I WAS RUNNING

Away in

The world unfathered

Unmothered my beloved

Far away

Arms were a cave

You could hide

In a fuck

Birds supping

On the worm

The sun had not

Yet set

It lit up

An aged woman's

Upper lip

Organizing itself

At length

About the gin glass

OLD MACDONALD HAD A FARM

Great sadness having been so long entranced
The OPEN sign blinks on and off

Dark-eyed person telling a beautiful alphabet
My sex is in me and my computer

Stretched into bands of white elastic
Light about the sun. I tried to write it down

A peacock's fan had opened in my eye
It brought me lovers I couldn't keep

And an intimation of evil like scent or
The surface of opaque water roughened

By a wind in the dark. I addressed
My addressee by the wrong name. He

Responded without acknowledging
My error. I invited myself over. He

Said Come. I had been handed a blinding
Blonde baby centaur at a wedding at an evil

University. Moving around the world
That fast left little need for drugs. Between

Sleep and wakefulness, estrangement
And one's sandals moving along a ground

One kind of food, then another kind, neutral
Declensions of what passes over wi-fi

And nobody could even remember what that
Was short for

DEAD SYMBOLISTS

The bell tolled a graceful
Interlude. I saw
A star above the point
Of a spruce in the brightening
Sky. Then it was gone. A bird
Sang in the courtyard. A man
Overtook me in Freedom
Square. You don't look
American, he said, I bet
You do a lot of squats. I saw
You walking back there.
It was true, I had been
Walking past a fruitseller's
Door hung with the crimson
And purple sticks of walnut
And grape mash that are
A Caucasian delicacy.
Caucasian is a strange euphemism
I heard a cat or a child
Yowling. A man in pink spoke
Sharply. Forks
Rattled in the next room
A woman with hennaed
Hair moved through
The dappled courtyard
A beautiful woman with painted
Eyes in a long black veil
Stood outside MARLEY
The head shop and electronics
Store under Pushkin Street

Leaves and spruces shone
In apricot light. A man
Was preceded by his enormous
Belly upon which a lit
Cigarette rested, stepping
Quietly out of the alley
Around six in the morning.
The gaping mouth of Stalin
Was flanked by two muscular
Men in profile opposite
The 24-hour grocery
A cat loped among
The chairs of SINGER,
A restaurant. A thin
Dog with out-turned legs
Had a coin-sized orange
Tag stapled to one ear
The man overtook me
I just want to talk to you
For a minute, he said
I swear I'm not crazy...

SCHISANDRA

Glad under gore.

—MS Harley 2253, "Ichot a burde in a bour ase beryl so bryht"

Millipedes, scarabs, jackals and dogs
And that was just the rug
Letting the book stay closed
My shaking aunt
Enter man in fit flops
Doing what comes naturally
Ratified by the passions that so eerily
Pass. And kissed the door
Post and the door. As the flame
Is bound to the burning coal
Or so it says in SEFER YETZIRAH
What does it really mean to lay
An egg? What is the significance
Of a nest or womb outside
The body? A woman is a man
Without a beard said Harbhajan
Singh Khalsa, better known
As Yogi Bhajan. Calligraphy
On the shell of the egg
Of a Common Murre
A trunk of sea opened
For the deep diver and the swallowing
Throat, the planets moaning
As they moved around
A bottle of "five flavor berry"
Capsules could be a natural
Source of energy at times
The parental membrane

Of your guiding cells flags
Maybe I resent you because
You don't know what it's
Like in the dark, because
Neither courage nor necessity
Ever led you there. "She
Told me that at Leavenworth
Not long before she learned
Of her commutation, a robin
Had alighted at her window
A small messenger from the world
Outside. Hadn't it been
A sign? She had taken it as one."
(THE LONG, LONELY
ROAD OF CHELSEA
MANNING, *NY TIMES*
JUNE 2017)

DISTINGUISHED SENTIMENTS

At least we know
That what we do
We do with feeling

                    or

In those days we knew it
Moving just slow
Enough to see the fault
Between whatever
It was we thought
We felt and the situ-
Ation then unfolding
In the sky. For there was
A difference
Even if and when we
And it rhymed. There
Was always the sense
That another thing

                              landscape

Could mean, could
Also mean, and its
History and old
Senses of nature or
Old sepses of persons
Their effluent disappearing
Into the mulch, sublime
Dagger teeth
Pinking the maw
Of devouring & so hospitable
Earth, was that what
Feeling we there

Apprehended was its not
Ours, that we weren't
In particular the ones
With the problems or
The sense of tragedy
Or even the seeming
Need for eloquent
Torques of black
Exhaust to make
Their unsayable
Glyphs disappear

                          again

Into the dying
Sky. That
Sentiments had
History
We knew
And that
The history
Of feeling up
Until that time
Had been put
Into books we
Also knew
The purchase
Of feeling
Was already
Very old then
Too. And yellow
Breeches blue

Waistcoat, beside
The point or just
One more factor
Of the color wheel
A menu
For all elaboration
Even the catalogue
Of scents & extracts
Exact science
Of all that still
Remains our
Inheritance
With which precious
Few were ever to
Become comfortable, one
More fact of living
On a ball
The molten salmon
And watermelon of all
Evening, eternal youth death
Of evening everywhere
At which time wherever
You were it was
Always still then
In those days the nineteenth
Century. We didn't
Have to make
Up any of it.
It awaited us
Here, as waited all

The rats in all
The crotches of the palms
And the caressing hiss
Wheels still made then
Ghosting the blanched
Wide roads when
The last white
Man drove West

NO CHILD LEFT BEHIND

There was no manual for holy women
& had there been one we would have torn
It up, if we're going to be honest with ourselves

& we do seek to be. Rapid
Maturing, forced tuning of our instruments
Moving through your city quietly & purposefully

Was it but an old commonplace
That god needed your eyes to see through
As you carried that child down the corridor

& bathed her carefully, just the way
You promised you would. Schools
For scammers were everywhere. You filled

Out a form to disqualify yourself
& another form for permission
To do things to what remained of the light

At the ecowarfare conference
As in other circumstances
Where the conditions for the end

Of us are enumerated
The gentle air above the speakers'
Heads & above ours

& about our bodies
& within us when we draw
It in circulates calmly, tactfully,

Peacefully

GIZZARD

I was in a bar in Albuquerque

I was going to have to sleep with somebody

I was going to have to choose between two men

It wasn't going to work with both of them

This blue-eyed man was very drunk

On leave from the army, big German

Bones in his face, he was telling me about his sex

Career. I didn't particularly want him

There were however things I wanted him

To tell me. He'd been at Mount Sinjar

After the massacres there. He wanted

To tell me about his marriage. I'm impotent

Now, he said, but I have chemicals (he was

An army chemist but he was referring

To Cialis which he said he preferred

To Viagra), and having never

Yet fucked a geezer on pills I wasn't

Totally uncurious how it all might

Go down. But this other

Man was supposed to be showing up any minute

On his motorcycle who was the hottest

Person in town I'd been able to find with my phone

I'd been living in a trailer on my friend's land

I had taken refuge with the lesbians

And their dogs. I had been dealing with a creep.

I had hardly seen a man

In going on two months. I just had to know if they

Were still there. Things had gotten to that point. Through

Great confusion must we make

Our way. A rare people practicing their ancient

Religion had recently

Been massacred by the Islamic State

On the mountain that was sacred to them.

This man had been there.

But I'd grown too drunk to engage

Him any further. It would have meant

Going to his room. I didn't want to.

I went with the other man, the one

I wanted, who didn't know anything

About what I wanted to know

I'd seen the iridescence

On the surface of spilled oil. I'd seen

Rainbows. Until the fan spread

Across my vision I had mistaken

Peacocks for decoration

Were they secretly Quetzalcoatl

The phoenix, guardians at the gates

Of Eden, were the gates of Eden

Depicted in the amber gates

That partly enclosed the many

Eyes in their tails, were they

Allegories for the heavenly

Panopticon or answers

To the feminine yearning to feel seen

And what about their ugly voices

Shameless horniness, and the legend

They copulate as follows:

The male weeps

The female licks his tears

SAFEWAY

RUNNING NYMPH

for Nicole Eisenman

I was on my knees
Hacking my brains
Alone in a bone

Of unratified light
Someone downstairs
Was retching

& up thru the airshaft blew a baconlike
Breeze with notes of weed & a colorless
Wave came down through the orange

Mesh the super put up to keep out the pigeons
& doves. They beat their wings. Something
Historical was happening to me

Something already
Antique. I felt myself pushing
My hair to one side of my face. I swear

     Society
Was making me do it
The voices

From the television reached me. They had
Had to pass through at least three walls.
They were like

Everything.
                    Everything
Overtakes me eventually

19 january 2017

WHO HERE UNDERSTANDS ENGLISH

In jeans by Isabel
Marant in two
Legs that I cross all
By myself I detect

The weird mayonnaise
Of one of my rage
Secretions battening
Down behind my fly

And my head bending
Over the feeling and my
Two arms like dead white arms
On the grid of this

Outstretched page   .
Thinking of my genius
Friends, my rapes, all
The guilt I feel

Everything that belongs
To me, first of all
My lack of faith, first
Of all my infidelity

To everything I've been
Shown. No, first of all
It's a blossoming, womanly
Feeling in the caves

Of my guts, bright
With lights & soda
Observing Canada
Geese pad across an ice rink

Like old people in bathrobes
Haven't figured out
How to talk to my father yet
Who here understands English

Still haven't figured out how to talk to my father

19 january 2017

BEAUTY

Je suis belle, ô mortels! comme un rêve de pierre
—Charles Baudelaire

These poisoned sensations have to be
Accepted if they're to be
Overcome. Looking
Up calories on my phone

Not that I'm counting
Don't even like numbers
It's something vestigial
It comes in bad minutes

To teach my body something's in control
Something little & unholy, wrong idea
Of information, chiseling a transparent minute
Into myself with the afterimage of a form

If I did this kind of thing
On the bigger machine it'd be
Worse. Worse
Things than this are bombing

The world. A terrible
Fate is coming to power tomorrow. I'm reading
The early poems of Sherman Alexie. Desolation
Of secular life. I remember the luxury of speculating

All mystical traditions grew up
In the souls of a disciplined few
Turned in on themselves while under
Occupation by tyrants. That was then. This

Morning I could see one comfort: to become rock
Hard. Could imagine one comfort:
To have become rock. I had no
Imagination. I had his. I had theirs. "Formalism

& grammar are ways to be thin..." masochism
Merely thought of, the idea of a calorie
Most boring way to feel womanly doing itself to me
This morning I was panicking, burning, I was desperate

Scanning the body of my bedfellow
Its beautiful cheeks & chin
& long smooth abdomen
My silence growing fat like an old fruit

Still making me sick
It makes me sick I longed
For the wrong thing
I longed for death. I dreamed of stone

19 january 2017

SKULL&BONES

I'm wearing a used fake
Fur coat like a cartoon
Ermine. I've belted
It with genuine
Snakeskin—
Blonde. I've eaten
Three eggs
With a fork, three
Strips of grassfed
Beef with my fingers.
A cookie with my fingers.
Didn't pay for any of it.
Couldn't. Didn't
Clean the pan.
Still hungry.
Not hungry at all.
Can't tell.
Had a little talk
With my lover.
Couldn't be avoided.
A few fat tears rolled
Off me. I kind of don't
Want to come
I said, or
I can't, I need
To but I can't
Come right.
Don't want to.
Also I can
Tell you've lost

Confidence when you
Touch me, I said. Kind
Of not in my body
Right now, beside
Myself, haunted
& sand
& infinity spread
Into my dreams
Emptiness throbbing
In me like an incarceration
Some trouble
I've seen
Desertification
Sand for the devil
I don't know.
Incarceration should
Never be used
As a metaphor.
That's
A feeling. Last
Night's dream is still
Going. Seeing
God hasn't saved me.
Wraiths of snow
Slavered over
The white highway.
We drove through gales
Blasting *La Traviata*
Wasting our brains dividing
The truth from kitsch

In the Lily Dale Bargain
Store, in the good
Bar just off Seneca land.
It was a whole day's labor
Reading where Geronimo's
Skull ended up and the lawsuit
That failed to move it.
Guess who owns the world.
I put away an hour
Reminding institutions to pay me
My income hasn't been
Regular enough for *that*
Kind of friendship this year. All
The people I miss
While I'm wound
Up in this. Opened
A fresh can for the cat.
Now I'm a person
Who does that. Woke up
Still dreaming of like three
People's feeds.
The world keeps forcing
Its way in. "The world"
Which fucking one.
You know the one.
And I was one
Of the lucky ones.

IN BLOOM

This is the time
And this is the record
Of the time
    —Laurie Anderson

I'm in the Sedona Safeway
Looking up "vortex" on my phone
What a scam. All Safeways
Call flowers "Poetry
In Bloom"   Last night
We camped in the rain
A psychic shook a bag of cowrie-
Studded discs onto a table & told
Me I'd get back my lost notebook
Mercury is in retrograde and you
Are on the road, he said. He looked
Like a LARPer. I liked what he had
Had to say about the holographic
Universe we're living in. I hadn't
Said it was a notebook missing, only
Something special to me. The man
Behind the counter at the New Age
Bookstore, flames on his shirt & a tasseled
Kerchief on his head & beads & gems
Around his neck, supercilious
In his periodic request that his patrons
Direct to him "any questions" couldn't tell us
Where to get mushrooms, or wouldn't. This
Is a conservative place he told me
Gesturing through the air around him
As in, Ask somebody else but watch out who.

I counted twenty white people shopping
For crystals & novels channeled
From the Pleiades near eight
PM on the eve of New Year's Eve
Speculating that people with money marry
People and produce offspring who then
Require elaborate healing. A whole
Story, or one entire way to tell it,
A coming-of-age tale, would simply
Describe the emergence of life into
Ugliness. That tale alone. The bad
Songs walking all over emergent life.
The smell of burning plastic. The loss
Of memory followed by the loss
Of its devices. But I meant no unkindness
To the channelers. Much less any
Toward the Pleiades. I thought how I hated
Myself—most available person—for five
Long years just for having seen
What I saw & sensing this was not a world
In which the truth could be told. Upon
Reflection it has scarcely ever been.
That once I saw a dancing star or saw
The black flame face of Gede
Inches from the face of Michel André
On his cracked balcony on Morne
Hercule near three PM in the shade
Of green leaves, I'd found
A religion on these facts but I have
To go to the bathroom... *cells... cells...*

Cells of spirit could be felt on the air
Each... with its own... personality...

EMERGENCY ROOM

Toothless man with a blackened toe screaming
I heard my blood screaming thru my veins
Like wind on a Sierra
Like electronic music
Elegant doctor in tight white
Coat, gray heels, bright
Pink complexion sways up
To me "where does it hurt, baby"
The old man has caused a commotion
Throwing off his coverings
Accepting nobody's touch
But I'm enjoying the "care"
The doctors & nurses all flirting
With each other, me
& my fucked
Up leg. I forgot
How much I love human places
Courthouses & hospitals
Gas stations & rest
Stops in the wee hours
New York in the dark when somebody's
Crying into their phone
Wherever
People are naked
Be nice, Papi, you gonna fall
Says a nurse
You have to sit up in the bed
Three beautiful medical professionals
Bending over him now
Papi be nice, why you fighting

He's gonna fall!
Siéntate
Human touch
Human care
Human beauty
Divine mystery

TRY NOT TO DISTURB THE LIVE PALMS

Try not to disturb the live palms

Do not oppress the paper flowers

Or the little birds crying

Or the fragrant mildews rising from the gloom

Or the painted sides of reeds

Dried reeds like the ones through which ant

People climbed up to the floor of the world

In the days when the sky was still so low

Even small men had to stoop when they walked

Whether or not they had come from an ape

It was dark. Little truths beguiling

And infinitesimal roughnesses diverting one idea

Or the next into matter, glottal stops, fine white

Hairs among the sheen on a neck nape in sunshine

Through which a breeze with no name has just passed

3 march 2017

WASTING AWAY IN THIS VANILLA DARKNESS

for CAConrad

Kegel now before the monarchs
Flutter up under the lamps to smoke
The guard coming toward us
Looks like Félix Morisseau-Leroy
Hurry the rest of them won't be beautiful
Like him. Metallic taste of old
Cherry Coke. These are the mechanic's keys
Don't move them. It happened
To be a moment I was feeling bad
About myself. We were in the souvenir
Kiosk behind the throne room
The arrow in my compass began
To quiver, solemn colonels slicing key
Limes into keys into a tureen of wastoid
Pukes lightly slapped with a platelety
Lasagna by the white hand of a handsome
Waiter in a battalion of balls
On a billiard table loaded w eternally
Tween thoughts reconstellating
The diamond sense of genocide's very
Worst ideas. It was like a portrait
Of happy people that you and I have
Certainly both seen. I was only
Trying to recover a sense of myself
I am not trying to be forgiven
For that I am just telling you
Strange bran steaming up from my genitals
Gems are the eyes of god said Julian

And how did birds begin?
VOID IF DETACHED
I came upon the ruins of a bird in a beet
Field in Normandy. I gathered them
Up & carried them quietly into Lithuania
I went into Lithuania very very quietly
& silently sleep stopped coming
Some of my family had escaped
About a hundred years earlier. I might
Have been the first to return. I hid
Everything I could recollect and also
What I could not behind my books
And I hid it behind my clothing and hair
Snowden was somewhere in the Moscow
Airport the day at Duty Free a Russian
Woman mistook me for a star. I'm
Not anybody famous I told her. She
Did not want to believe. The forests
Looked like a big black boar
Capital had a different way of flowing
It seemed to mean a new
Virulent strain of heterosexuality
A lot of striptease bars, Zaras & sex
Clubs, shining black caviar, lurid orange roe
The rainbow spread across the surface of whatever
Spilled. It shone on the mallard's neck. And all over the crow.

CÉLEUR

You are speaking into posterity

And beautifully

Glissant

But as for the whiskey called Buffalo

Trace. But as

For spirits I

Mean spirit epitaphs

One mouth dick

Is fucking its head's other

Mouth. It's a metaphor

For silence. It's not

A metaphor at all

NO WORDS

I lost my notebook maybe

A week ago now. I couldn't

Put that into words till now

"No words" said the subject

Heading of an email from Cecile

Richards of Planned Parenthood

I can't even

Said my feed

Yas Queen

Preach

Glottal stop

Glottal stop. Shit emoji said

Some guy aloud. That psychic in Sedona

Said I'd get it back

He was wrong. Red

Mud on my blonde boots

Ordinary people shouldn't

Be allowed to do drugs

I conclude remembering

Ruefully my ecstasies

In front of the damning

Evidence of a Burning

Man book. Some birds

Overhead spilled into

The sky like a fistful of ashes

I wrote down the word THROVE

When Colm Tóibín read it

Through Bluetooth to

The rented Chrysler's

Speakers as we crested

A hill with a future

Anterior prayer in me

To have thrived

NIGHT IS FALLING

for Bett Williams

My cheek was covered in sores
My friend came to Safeway
Waited in the car while I paid my phonebill in a bodega
Waited in the car while I bought makeup
Drove me to her friend's house in Joshua Tree
A sexy little woman in a cowboy hat and boots
She made a living writing for *Marie Claire*
& had recently experienced an intriguing assignation
On Mount Shasta with a tall, weatherbeaten
Mind reader but now I must close for
Night is falling over Desert Center

HUNTED BY A SINGLE THOUGHT

Felt something rising in me
Tamped it down with food
In the irradiating air
Stretching out, elongating
My tiny fate
Like a scarred & oblong
Pore, stretching out the little
Ditch I dug in my consciousness
Hunted by a single thought
The gouging tooth of beauty
Sinking in

QUEENS

for Yva Tapia

First part of the wicker of un-understanding
Ne plus ultra of asshole boyfriends
Who was trying to pull my arm
I fell heavily to sleep with jellyfish
In my stomach, there had already
Bean a curious headache of nuts, deep
Decay of death & unholiness, then a high
Neighbor speakerphoning with a woman
All night. He goes BRRRRRRRRP and
DRRRRRRRRRRRRT with his mouth
When he is aroused. You know why I like you
He speakerphones on the stair. You
Notice every little thing about me.
Then in the night my friend across
The hall cried out MY FRIEND
IS DEAD & there was a commotion
& the matriarch downstairs shouted
Her men back into the house screaming
I'M LOCKING THE DOOR, THE COPS
ARE COMING. Then police and paramedics
Filled the building and their whirling red lights.
They carried the neighbor down in a chair.
I heard him talking so he wasn't dead
In bed now in a stocking cap and a button-
Down shirt. CHEESEBURGER
IN PARADISE it says. We wanted to be close
To each other. I wanted to feel people
Living. I wanted to live too. The gate
On the building slamming closed

I tell myself I'm sitting here unmolested
Then I remember the night J got arrested
After a bird chirped between movements
Of Mozart's Mass in C

JOSEPH'S DREAM

Mike Pence was wearing
A lavender workshirt
He was leading a yoga
Class.
I was in it. A teacher's
Insecurities are always
Apparent. "That's the fifth
Stupid thing I've done today,"
Said Mike. It was only the first
Stupid thing I'd noticed him do
Absenting myself from hell
In downward dog I saw
The social role of the future
For men like him

WOMEN SEEM LIKE A LABOR

He was doing that diet where you eat a brick
Of Irish butter. Women seem like a labor
To convince someone anyone of something
At all times. A kind of dusty tawny dried
And greenish pelt. Looking at the small
Colors starting to emerge
From under the surface of your arms
You would have gone somewhere but
In those days there was no escape rounding
The bend of the globe—you could maybe
Say something—or sustain a kind of
Alkalinity eating whatever it was you were
Supposed to be eating. You could have
Sex if you still wanted to. You could even
Romanticize it. The tools were still freely
Available. You could do things to your
Appearance and get to work on weaponizing
Any aspect of your experience you could rouse
Yourself to witness. Oh and you were free
You were absolutely free to have Experiences
Of Art

THIS IS THE SONG OF ONE HUNDRED

This is the song of one hundred
Thousand chemicals approximating
Sunshine in my hair. My lover bit
My cheek this morning. I think I'll
Fall from one trance into the next
Might fall asleep any minute
It gets tiring making yourself look
Like you're alive while you're looking
Hard practicing turning
Away from the shit we're in

EQUIMO

Colors parachuting down from the sky
Like opals with puffs of rose moving over
Them like smoke. Dreamed I saw a tweet
Condemning the disavowed patrician whiteness
In the poetry of John Ashbery, "the great,
Relaxed curve of time" neighbor dragging
His slippered feet across the floor
I was climbing up a hill to the radio station
It was spring and overcast, clouds rose
At the edges. The woman radio host
Was really a girl. I could feel her desire
She went on break. I sewed something
For you she said, laying them in an unfrilly
Pile. Back outside the sky was now blue-gray
Walking down the small-town hill
It could have been Belgium it might have been
New Jersey. I sacrificed the rest
To J's suave body, dense and smooth
Like the child of a moon and a horse

THE SHOT HEARD ROUND THE WORLD

for Anne Waldman

How long does it take a revolution to arrive?
We weren't waiting anymore. It had happened
And yet it still hadn't arrived. It was
An experience of dryness—
"An experience of the abyss" I might write
It was a wooden revolutionary ski lodge
Fillets of verse, the triumph of the word
Waking up dry with a hangover headache
Nathalie touched my sores thru the mask
It was a revolutionary conversation (I guess)
I had been given a seat at the table
But I didn't want to sit at it
The blues were brewing, drying out
My tongue. "I took a course on doing
Things with time" said Leonard Cohen
In my dream in perfect iambic pentameter.
Today will be false spring. I already ran out
Screaming I DISAGREE
WITH THE QUESTION

REPORT

Without headphones without
Book. At once muscular
And carbuncular & wearing
A dress that could only
Be called Hulk Hogan I went
To the meeting. Because
I had to. Because not to
Could have only been called
Maladaptive. Well what kind
Of poet were you the people
In power demanded to know
In so many worlds. An around-
The-world poet I guessed. Two
Fresh pink boys had moved
Down the block. I'd
Seen them in their college
Sweatshirts on my way
To the train, with the rubbery
Haunted look of sheltered
Youths before whose eyes
Many decapitations and porns
And little else of moment
Has passed. Much to await
From such bright youth

YOU KNOW WHAT COMES NEXT

The sun was falling on a long scar

Of tar. We were driving north

I thought I'd stopped bleeding

But I was wrong. A fine confetti

Of late blood dusted all three

Rest stop toilets. It snowed

Toward Buffalo it got bright

And very cold. The skin

On my arms grew white

And crepey. I was being

Made to have makeup

Applied. Lena

Dunham was overburdened

With cat duties. "They"

Wanted her changing

The litter just too much. These

Were conditions of the soul

I tried each thing wrote John

Ashbery. You know what

Comes next who are watching

TV. I was trying to remember

How to live. Why do they

Say "stepped foot." Dreamed

I went to sleep on a traffic

Island in Djibouti.

"I was trying to find

My voice" she moaned

Do it with your male

Style genius I mean

Your fat stylus I

Mean whatever

You can find

THE SONG WITH THE REFRAIN LIKE ANIMALS

I was raising

My eyebrows for

No reason entering

The subway having

Composed my face

Into a state

Of intellectually

Curious alarm

Of hospitality

To the other

And caution

And but

And but also

Caution

And unsurprised

Yet not uncompassionate

Shock

MISUSE OF GIFTS

It's like a forty
Year old white
Man's poem
Misuse of gifts
I heard the sirens
I saw their allures
Sick girl surrounded
By barrettes and magazines
Halting in the throat
Like a latent planet
Hung in the air
Like a lamp
In a basement
Like a bomb
Over your country
Combing the snow
Leopards for one
That would look
Back at their camera
Scarily close to the border
Between the desert
And the city

DAYS OF OUR LIVES

Solemn sandal subtracted
From the foot of Mohammed
Wants to call itself witness
Inside your dream
The dead feeling was long
And boring
Of great capacity
Devouring engine
Of democracy
Swallowed the sacred
Feeling the lump
In your throat

CHAPS

in memory of Sam See

Can you turn toward it
A smell
Can I believe in
Such measure
Breathless
Breathlessly sad
Ebb of
All life
We knew it
Would come
Sick of this
Consciousness
A braid
My mother
Fingers drying
Down
Coldest spring
Of the year
Voluptuous
Piece
Of stone
I would rather
Bow to rocks
I will take
Your abstract
Smile
Pure & virile
Ancient history
The flame face

Pocked wall
Slow sleeve
Of trance-
Inducing
Exercises
Falling from
It one by one
The room
Was cold &
Clear, a hard
Metal parody
Of classic
Japans
Something
Failed to find
Me there
A tortoiseshell
To see through
A breathlessness
Unwitnessed
Born to lose her
Arms closing
Over
A kind of soot
No one could
See the smug
Closed ibex
Mouth the sound
Of such
A voice

I want to
Do it I think
I want to do it
The word dolor
Squat cop entering
CHAPS too
Lubricious a name
For a bagel
Store photograph
Of magnolia
Obscured by a
Lamp

ENLIGHTENED DESPOTISM

It must be the full
Moon making me
So round she wrote
Predictably. Less
Room under that
Sweatshirt there.
Bra cutting into
The back. You
Look very pretty
Today Miss says
A man outside
The deli. Adulthood.
As though she
Were somebody's
Mother. Or it
Was more conceptual
Than that: the *idea*
Of motherhood was
All a softening body
Would now swallow
& arrange itself around
Was she to remain
Afraid of pleasure, sugar
Bread, fucking, forgetting
The struggle, forgetting
The real drama at hand
Body and face built
To prevaricate forever
In the enlightened

Despotism of some
Mind you could replenish
At will via PayPal

BEEF BACON CHICKEN AND NUTS

Beef bacon chicken and nuts
Are already revolving in my guts
Like ancient women in vacant lots
"The first false spring is here"

I'm always hungry. Dinosaur
Jr. Wore my dimpled thighs out
With my hair. These are bad
Times. Everybody says so.

Everybody knows. Collapse
Of the age of the virtuoso
Somebody's history told in hairs
The words between the lines

That are not there. Another
Spring, the fruit outside a store
In foreign states. I don't even
Know what she did with such charisma

And such need. Spare ribs appeared
Twice in a single volume of short
Stories, shadows groaning long
Across the day. We lay

In bed and the birds got loud
Somebody made a meme with lines
Of mine and said so in the putting
Forward of oneself via self-loathing

We've all been using. Even the ones
Who do it best make me sick
Alive to it
But I'm still hungry

PARTICIPLES OF DESERERE

u let me pluck leaves
from yr hanging-down beard
clover gemmed with rain
wet acacias fragrancing the fine
young palms the mosses wet
over careful sons of julian complicating
my arousal   the care i feel for this
creature unbombastic   its fever now
making it tread quietly across the floor

      virgin moss
          virgin bloom
      revirginated forests boreal
      pregnancy apogee of the virgin annunciation
      full fathom five thy father lies

hawk red on a streetlight
sun temple in the form of a chariot
lariat grasses tender & green
leaves unshaven beards of rain
cooked chocolate
sun in mounds
i used my best bitch voice
to get more ceviche for tongo's
mother arlene   just
back from six months in venezuela

             "cow's mouth
salivating in the street" tongo's
poem

strange car with its butt cut off
window selling a new blonde espresso
conspiracy born of the president's hair

looking at pine boughs
thinking up money
passing santa teresa boulevard
pines circusing the dark clouds
bolaño's cheek as turning light
on a distant hill   faint rainbow before us

a note from the beautiful sculptor
email promised from smoky glasgow
polar ice screaming into water
tongo's lines   past the xmas tree grove
glowing jane & bright layla
a palm beside a pine
unspooling the father's iridescent petroleum
green moss on all the ropes of trees

past the garlic of gilroy
clots of nopales & signs
for cherries   hill covered
in yellow mustard flowers
& despairing of the instruction he craved
he withtook himself again to questing lines
rain drove down on bending cows

8-tracks of kalipooni
teacher awakened by a rat
spectres of our supposed collective
wickedness   the lenten
technocratic churches of norcal
rain misting the wild highway
gasoline of the twentieth century
pooling at watsonville
where j once   in the car with a pathological
liar   saw a flying saucer

in the cold white light of my computer
my client called me a genius
cadence of twentieth-century alibis
cadence of gentle men to
whom i now loose my pen
it was just one way of keeping the promise
once made to me that i could be a hundred
thousand people   nausea
at the sight of our flag
too big in the blowing rain
guns in the quiver of the state
tear gas eardrum destroying machinery
the gun of wrecked children the AR-15

a partial history of iridescence
gizzard like an abalone hid
among giblets in the holiday bird
day of mourning from hurricane
sandy to sandy
hook   stand of trees

in the form of china
the great sand fire of 2016
hot wind over the water at big sur
jonah down in the whale
alien song chiming the trident seas

moon cloven by abyssal birds
twilight must be the darkest
hour on the highway, she sang
but tho her song rang true
it was not so

almost upon the sorrows
of coalinga where svp's "sexually
violent predators" are locked
in their hospital where cows
go to die   past soledad
the crime   with the beautiful name

industrial death from which all souls recoil
upon which we still sup
tongo said the oakland juvie broke him
boys locked in closets ringing the indoor yard

virgin moon
untouched by god
& man   a buddha
dream   everyone wearing a topknot
"you've already covered all the material"
bitter incarcerating angel

all my self-cruelty or my liver
accomplishing the churning
of waste into shit
whatever i did for guilt or duty
whatever i exchanged
for a brief anesthetizing season
in unthreatening beds

"pigs for sale"
"freedom is not free"
worm moon
moon of primeval emergence
virgin navel pressing out into the world
up from the wet soil
up from the ground
green eating glacier water
i don't know that you ever set foot in california
gentle scholar, searcher, poet
finder out of the secrets hid in "junk" dna
entertainer of the wilder ideas
true weaving, true intelligence, all gifts inadmissible
to the university, data uncorroboratable
virtues incomprehensible to high court
gifts of years conferred in a single spoken word
mystic radio of galena & clay
& other ingredients i cannot say
rubbed on the heel of the palm
& presented to the rising sun

ARMORICA

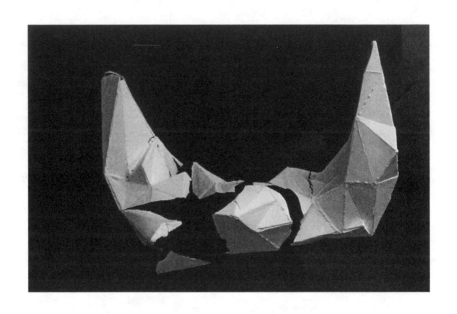

She had almost mastered it

It was nothing she

Had not

Felt before

False peace of my adulthood

She thought

Behind her smile

False peace of my art

Moving toward the true

The secret peace

Nothing she had not

Thought before

Her teeth drying in the air

Barely at the beginning

Of falsehood

I'm smiling she

Thought

Greeted suddenly by her next-

Door neighbor, transubstantiating

Mere recognition

Into pleasure

Just barely falsely

It was only she'd been lost

In her thoughts driving absently

To the grocery store

Then already parking there

Or somehow already parked

Unconsciously when the woman

Her neighbor arpeggiated

Against the window

Of the car polished

Nails she rolled the window

Down

Smiling

Oh hi I didn't realize you were there

How long had she been sitting there like that

Still smiling, the neighbor's

Skirt swirling behind her as the electric

Doors opened

Now it was time to adjust

Her mouth back down

Suddenly seeing the constant grin

Of her bones behind the flesh

As the feeling of duty at last

Began to wither

She remembered her daughter

Buckled into the seat behind her

Her smile took its time going down

Her face would not release it

Or she felt the familiar space

And looseness, the sense of wide

Incompletion in reality

That old familiar feeling

She had felt since she herself

Was four

As her daughter unbuckled her

Own seatbelt and offered

Her two arms for her mother

To lift her up out of the car

And carry her into the store

For she still didn't like to let

Her walk even holding hands

Across the parking lot

The woman at the cash

Register (she still called it cash

Register in her mind, why, almost

Nobody carried cash anymore) had the same

Name as her mother

Few enough people in the store

At that hour

Bright chrome bank of wheeled carts

A fine mist spraying the greens

The ghost of her smile minutely

Still haunting her like a glare held in

Behind the eyes once they've closed

And some dagger slid in there

In what she'd left open in her feeling

Some dagger hid there

A presentiment or memory of things

That happened here before she ever

Set foot here, and the things done to her

And the things done to other women

Whatever she turned into the smiles

She stretched across the gulf

Of the more and more and ever

More she could not say

Nothing she meant to make a big

Deal of, only some tiny budging

Of memory, the sense of duty hidden

Inside her body, that willed her

Transubstantiate it all, and the aggrieved

Look of the woman working out opposite

Her this morning, a wholly ancient

Look of ritual death, of sacred sacrifice

Of readiness to die right then

For the truth, and she wondered did her

Face too release such overwhelming

Longing and such arresting intimacy

With agony

With things no matter what you tell

And no matter what you do

Your body will protect

And keep

And knit into its very flesh

Where else could that

Woman release her feeling

Than the socially acceptable anguish

You could get for twenty dollars at CoreBarre

Earlier that morning a square

Of sun spreading like a melting

Pat of butter across the dark hair

Of her lover, into whose body

She could no longer hide her need

For worship, it had grown too

Familiar, almost like a child's now

In its need for her and almost like

Her husband's

Across town running his record

Company out of their garage

Their daughter before her now

Dandled in the seat of the cart

And facing forward not toward her

Because that's what the child

Preferred

This still strange sensation of falsity

She had felt it hundreds of times, the descent

From a daydream into the real

Dispersion of a thought she

Could almost see, giving way

To produce and fruit

Certain knowledge

She was no longer starving

Artist as mother she thought
A book she might have seen
And that as long as she lived
Her daughter would not starve

Loss of herself

She still longed for it

Genderless self

Loveless and avid

Fearless, beyond care

Belly quivering against the light

Nipples too hard behind her sweater

Polished concrete floor

Making a living from the state

Of constant vigilance

She had perhaps misnamed

Liberty, she had perhaps

Mistaken for valiance

Though she would never share

Such self-cruelty professionally

Not with her dealer, herself

A brilliant woman and certainly never

With her passionate young

Students, but the staving-

Off of some long-domesticated

Appetite she was now

(For the thousandth time) conscious

Of translating into shopping

For vegetables

As she read the word SHOOTING

Absently with her left

Eye

Blood shooting silently
Into her brain

Her umbilical cord had been cut

As had been cut the cord of her daughter

These were not hidden truths

But she felt herself suddenly grave

As though at the bottom of a begging bowl

A crucible with a flame under it

Cooking her, her and her

Offspring on the floor

Of the grocery store, making their salts

And minerals turn and pop

Her singing daughter in the cart

Loaded with the chards and lettuces

Into which she'd bury most of what

She'd earned that week

Buried inside of which the obscure

Universally acknowledged medicines

Of the age and the even more occult

Calculus of the future, her daughter

Singing, head starred by that old

Barrette, and this fresh

Killing now spreading through her body

Up through her left hand

The hand that would not put

Down the phone and through

Her left eye, the one slightly

Dominant, incompletely

Rounded and never quite made

Whole by her years at the potter's

Wheel and an old

Concupiscence gnawing

At her root now, behind her well-

Cut jeans, legs parted as though

Before the wet clay on the wheel

As they would be later that

Day, but now the pulse

Throbbed there like the old doctor's

Rubber hammer had against her

Cold knee when she was a girl

Standing upright before her shopping

Cart she told herself, I am a free woman

Pursuing the good in a bad regime

As her blood broke the walls of all her veins

Seeping back into the chambers

Of her heart, its stern, proud

Walls, and the incarcerating

Angles and the cannibal angels

Obscurely making money off her

Kale and off the sale of bullets

Her dull white feminism, report

Of gunfire causing a branch

To tremble

And the blue fly

On the branch trembled with it

And she was moved

By a longing to hug her daughter

A longing she resisted

Lest the little one feel too keenly

Her mother's desolation and willingness

To lay her sorrows down upon the child

Some dagger slid in there

Some dagger hid there

She was aware of her smile as

"Feminine" and for a second forgot

Her own name. She was smiling

Again.

She was pushing

Her cart across the polished

Concrete floor, phone
Balanced in her left
Hand, why had she left
It in her hand, fingers too
Good at including it in the other
Things she did when she did
Anything other than work
But no she was at checkout now
And before she'd even read
The words she was only
Barely at the beginning of
Conscious of taking in
The shooting made her blood
Move in a new way
It shot her blood down
Into the ground

It was nothing

She had not felt

Before. It was a form

Of shame.

Why is this all I can think

Of she thought, her hand now

On the girl's cool brow

In Florida another child

Had murdered seventeen children

She learned

Through the cracked

Device she held in her left

Hand. She put rainbow

Chard and arugula and fennel

And spinach and kale onto the conveyor

Belt and chewable vitamins and advanced

Beverages friendly to the flora

In the human gut and the local

Craft beer her husband liked

It was the fourteenth day

Of February 2018

THURSDAY

Thurgood Marshall
Uma Thurman
Thelma Golden
Thor
Sir Thomas More
Thor
Heavy One
Sky Man
Thor's day
Thor

Jupiter
Jupiter
Jupiter
Jupiter

Bring me my gold
My serpent my rod
Pour hot gold into my teeth
Bind my silver tongue
Soak it in soft white gold
Jupiter
And unbind my tongue Jupiter
And loose it on the world

Alice ordered me to be made
But Alice doesn't live here anymore

Your tongue is in my mouth
I will suck you through the god in my mouth

He lives in the back
I am his student

I will suck you through the god in my mouth
Whatever man you say you are

I will suck the woman out of the man
Ferrying my wishbone across the top of the lip of my blood gender

Who lives in the back
Who lives in the black shine of my mouth

Your tongue is in my mouth Michael
I will suck you through the god in my mouth Aaron

Your tongue is in my mouth Alice
I will suck you through the god in my mouth Alice

Alice ordered me to be made Thurston
But Alice doesn't live here anymore

Warm milk chest
Heart tattoo in black box
White muscle pink nipple
Your tongue is in my mouth
You are a man
Mister little

Muscle man
Mister little angry man
The hair is black and stern across your forehead
This gristle fuck when your lips hang red over me
Ari you're my fantasy
You are telling me
You are always telling me this
I am to be the woman of this
Into me you press your purple red fist
Anciently as you like to say
I suck pearls whole out of your hard core

And seeing is believing
And I am dying to believe

Your tongue is in my mouth

I died our baby
I did it anciently
I couldn't help it
Bleed out on the wood sleeping me
I couldn't try
I couldn't do
The blood shamed me
It soaked me through
Clotting my sluices
Falling them up to the stars

Your tongue is in my mouth
The ceiling is in the cathedral

There I said so
The roof of the mouth of the cathedral reddening the way day dies
Ribbed in stone and painted blue
In hard gold zodiacs

Upon which I am soaked in black Roman water
Upon which I am doused in gray Greek water
Upon this sarcophagal brick of old black water

It is Thursday

Your tongue is in my mouth

Why am I eating so much cereal
I guess I wish it were morning
I want it to be morning already
I could put on Peace Piece tomorrow
Be night
Gnarled hands of oak
Like copper dusted with night dust
Shaking like the hands of remonstrant crones in my windowlight
Justice in the hands of oak
Jupiter oak
Thursday
Jupiter oak
Thursday
Jupiter oak
Thursday
My belly is empty on Thursday

And I am scared
I am scared
Stiff
Scared stiff
Scared to use words the way the lord uses them
Scared to hide in the burning bush
And call your name
And make you do what I want you to do
And force you to believe in me
Oak tree
Dead hand
Copper flame crone hand
Hag herbalizing and scrying the dark

Just past the edge of town in my hag hut
I drop a wiggling toad into the pot
I stir the smoking magic stew
I say the words like a poet

Here speaks a man of high fidelity
I draw a window with a high white sash
This window lives in The Portrait of a Lady
By Henry James which requires my fidelity
Which vision of a scandal lady like John Singer Sargent

I say what I see
This is my power

This is a snake of cars in a city that's stupid to me
This is how I shake my hair over what I care for
This is how I keep a secret
This is how I put words in your mouth

There is a small man standing up for himself inside me
I am a small woman standing up inside a tall man
In the world of persons god lives in the black of mouths
Something spoken by this god is every god in even the worst words ever
    spoken
The lisps of death in every mouth
I have no choice but to bless you
The lord commanded that I circumcise you
The lord commanded that I circumcise my mouth
I'm on all fours losing my baby
I'm on all fours in the universal hieroglyph of prayer
That's how we fucked in the days of Sumer
That's how we did it in the days of Sumer
That's how we make love in the days of today
Let's just say I want to be drenched in love
Sky man or gravity
Gravity and grace

We whose mouths are vases of god
Black god shines gold out of the red vase mouth light
We are vases of god in universal night

I don't care if you think I don't know what I'm saying
I know what I'm saying

The universe is moral

I frighten even myself
Is the name of carpentry
I wish the violence in me to die with myself
Is the work of carpentry

I have a woman's heart
Is the name of poetry
My cock is so huge it touches my woman's heart all the way
Is the work of poetry

This month I have had four lovers
I have had real love for them
I hope never to see them again
I will hang latent in the dark like a bat

And hoot like an owl to hunt them dead

At the edge of my mouth I am an old man
At the front of my mouth I am a girl
I bite down on a horse tooth with my yellow rat's teeth
Mild tooth of milk
Wild tooth of wolves
At the edge of my mouth I am an old man
At the front of my mouth I am a girl
Black n Mild like a cigar in a jar
Like a Cinderella made entirely of hair

When we fuck in the rafters
We are making love under the eaves
I saw a picture of Ashton Kutcher
Clutching Demi Moore's knees
He looked so disgusted and bored
Her toenails were painted crimson and literally terrifying
You could feel their isolation like a ray
Everything disgusting about love is an infection I have experienced personally
Everything glorious about love also belongs to me

Witness me as I draw this X
Everything your eye touches is the content of your kingdom
The crown slides down over my eye
The world exposes its egg to the Sky man
It will be Thursday again
Ashton's skateboard face and Demi's skull face will be bathed in severe sun
People Magazine will go up in flames

The blood stands tall in my veins Michael
I do not love you anymore Aaron
I like you Joey you don't know me at all
Alice you were never mine

Inserting fat into my head via my mouth
Inventing false anatomy with my new mouth
God lives in the back
Cruel February
The black hair is straight across your forehead
A curl is bad on my brow
Gingerly and with fidelity you are so loved by men
What's it like to be a man so loved by men
To be looked up to by them in this masculine way
Do you know who I'm talking to
When I say I and you say you

The blood stood tall in my veins
The sun touches me here in the place I've named for you
And falls back
Your impossible curling eyes of the sweet
Soft column behind the opening there
Where stars whittle their legs like little workers
And brush the fronds of my inner air
And sleep

I can see the Red Sea
It drains inside me

It parts
It drowns your severity Aaron
It drowns your cruelty Aaron
It drowns the evil book you throw at me
It drowns the knives in your muscle belly
It waters the teeth in my head
I can see the Red Sea
It drains me down to the abalone
It drains me down to my white-blue intestine
It swallows my chariot
You can't love me like that
I don't want it anymore
And also I've had enough murder and drugs
I have seen enough on these snake-white walls

Alice ordered me to be made Thurston
But Alice doesn't live here anymore

A paste of sand goes brackish in my veins
Dryer sheets in my throat
Rich people
Dead people
People whose heads emanate nothing
I got bored in February
I missed something so hard it made me sad in a final way

Today it is Wednesday
Tomorrow is Thursday
Then comes the day of rest

They told me I have to marry Mercury
You know they do that in Haiti
I am writing a book called Mercury I told them
Well you see, they said, that's excellent. But
You have to marry Jupiter too
They said. I do? I said, I do? I can marry two?
I even have to?
You have to they said
We will make you the rings
This one with the snake is for Jupiter
I don't know anything about him I said
But I do like the ring
I don't know anything about him I said

Don't worry they said
He knows all about you

Something soft is brushing my milk drape
Why does my body have to change for the light
I don't know how to do it
Thurgood Marshall
Thornton Wilder
Uma Thurman
Sir Thomas More
I don't know how to do it
Worship the god of persons
Worship the god who lives in the back
Feed him my food
Surrender all my names to him
Learn the difference between myself and another
I browse the curds and the grasses
I eat them with my muzzle
I am a cow like Rumi
I am a holy man
I have no idea how to do it
Holy holy holy
Nevertheless I have no choice but to do it
Holy holy holy man

Once you are in the car
You are on the road
Once you are on the road
You are the fool on a spool of God
Your existence flames in a scroll of sun
And here you are born
And here you are born again

And here you will ascend into the black mouth of God
I don't know how to do it but I am fuck well doing it
I am doing it
That's life I guess

Of course it can be secular to be alive on a Thursday
And as a matter of fact
It cannot
And as a matter of fact this is between you and me universally
And nothing I say belongs remotely to me

Only one grass whistles out the tooth of my horse
And the moon drops fast behind the fences
And the wheat lolls back
And waits for death

I could see the sea from where I was
My mesh hat shone blue

The jagged cheek of Gibraltar
Solid, sucked in the mouth and never melting
Where my dog's warm underleg soothes the whetstone
I speak of it thusly
I say it thusly
I lisp its name into the curl of wall stained dark in the impression of my
    mouth

Only one grass whistles out the tooth of my horse
And the moon bends back
And the wheat lolls back
And opens its stomach
And waits for death

I soak it in my black water
It seethes in bags I have hung up among the rafters
It seethes in bags of amber and jasper transfusions
Flower liquids in cellophane pouches
Streaked with goo clots of plastic soldier sun

When the pitcher is poured out the length of my tongue
And ten vats of grease ignite in unison

Only one grass whistles out the tooth of my horse
A too-tight phylactery
The moon bending back
The wheat lolling back
Scrollboxes clattering on the stone
Jugs of gasoline and jugs of sand

I threw my coat on the sea
The velvet sea
My coat spread
My coat spread
It was the blue of the top of the column of milk
Its soaked embroidery
It was the ditty two winds whined into the anus of night

Skating along the floor of the brook
Are leaves and ice. Devolving on the brook floor
It is only one little one. One blue shard of pale Palestine.
The wineskins are pricked
Goats' udders banged sore
Where mica lodges in the mucus house

Where my velvet is sucked down
Where the cheek blows thick with sleep to be brushed by the sea
Blue Palestine
Wrung swan neck in oil
Tasseling dirty day with rocks that fly and fly and fall and fall and fall.

The moon bends back
And the wheat lolls back

A cracker whitens on the tongue of the hanged man
My velvet is sucked down the sea
The seawall is chipped blue
The clock of Palestine
Gulls' salt beaks
Iron drums soldered shut and stuffed with salt cod
An anvil of rammed earth in the form of a baby belly button
Hair raised on the hat of the imperatrix
Embossed forever in her brass annal

No grass screams against the foot of my horse
No rock whinnies down the side of the sea
No scroll staves off the reeds quivering in my rib wall
And no algaes quiver
And no frogs belch out the tablet over the song of my purchase of night
Blue Palestine
Red sucker bloody on the bib of the world
Blue Palestine
Ice tray soaked in solid sun

14 february 2012

THE SADDEST YEAR
OF MY LIFE

CONFESSIONAL POEM

I expected the world would respond to my thought
I had seen some ads
I had been to their school

Forgive me
I didn't know where to turn
I didn't know where to look

Do not forgive me
For I did know, but I couldn't bear it

sent by hand

THE SADDEST YEAR OF MY LIFE

1.

i was crouching over my phone
waiting for it to tell me what to do

in that breast-swelling town
where a gray haze sprouts over the lips

of the water trailing a chemical film all over
her stepping dripping from the shower

nobody asking after the green
ivy hiding everything behind the alley

yesterday i stumbled
over a bear foot

Nefertiti corners of the mouth of Joan Baez
do you even remember

going to bed with the wrong man
sorrow slackening around him

i don't believe in the possibility of the wrong
man for i am the woman, the wrong one

watching the mute mattifying gentleness of those spruces
he is waiting for the morning

he awaits his morning feeds
an indoor man

extrusions
my fits

sick of turning my senses away
something necrotic behind the skin of the lower thighs

blacking out the world

2.

Nostalgia
               Portugal
Cup with J
               T-shirt
Football
               And I would
Of the neoliberal
                    Art performance
Game. In a Portuguese
                       Potato and they will
And spherical
               Like the earth
A certain slender Iberian
                     "sick muse"
Or another
               Forfeiture. Decline

3.

I forsook my dreams but they came back
For me like a scum I could never despise
Enough, missed appointments, theological
Thirst, a feeling of freedom
Experienced to spite my presence
Visible magnificence
Very fast, floating in my belly
I perceived a burden
Peruvian
A beautiful poet
Avenues
Who did as I pleased, or my dreams

4.

When I	personally
Closed	form. I can
Form	that
Clouds	to uncover the
Man	ring
His	little finger

thick like a horse's deep dimple

screwed me

5.

virginating
with my head
extracted yesterday's
mange
took & gave mange
under the sun
aura thickening

6.

I crawled
      You do
Inwardly
      So
        much
But in
To weather
remonstrances

It loved
      His glasses
      Curls
      Dinner & gin

Charging
Derelict yard
white pommel
the same tongue laboring laboring

7.

first the beards were there
then the berries were there

ankles and docks
a crust of glass

licking the glass
windows in piles

stacks of white casement
she threw back the sash

a synthetic
plush

it could mark you
it's not a mulch

it is the red
afraid of being pushed

across the border
where agrippa was waiting

he had become disorganized
scrolling boots by opening

ceremony and where was i
i was there

i was there and i
i too had begun to cling

to little pieces of trash

CUCURRUCUCÚ PALOMA

Googling Guerlain Baby
Glow over my beef
Carnitas in Whole
Foods a few hours
After my miscarriage
Prince died

TO LIVE IN A JEWEL WAS BLISS

Long pocket beside the wang
Of the man before me on the train
Did people still say wang or dong
Were those our parents
Sounding so wrong
Face in device light
Wondering if music
Still had the power
People seem to like a faux
Fur. Parts of the city were like
A jewel and parts were like hell
Selling red bags of poison white
Seeds, well-cut bangs on our
Slender young playwright
And her Massachusetts scrubbed
Of evil. Then a rock
Star texted me a pic of her
Vagina. To live in a jewel
Was bliss

INNER LIFE

Those tweets I sent about Duke Ellington
While my mom was being evicted again
According to what ethics under the sun
Can I possibly have been speaking? A
Kind of private feeling I can't even place here
Like a rock on a tomb or the thank-you
Gift of a guest whose plane leaves long
Before dawn

I feel the little school of minnows
In me changing direction, wavering
Pieces of consciousness eloquently
Describing to me giving up on the thought
Of ever reaching you

Then setting to feeding
On something closer by
An approximation of what
We could have had
One that asks less
Of me. One that asks nothing
Of you.

I put the device back in my pocket & keep walking

HEGELING BEFORE THE GLASS

I'll tell you something about being dead
It's boring
And it takes forever
Under dingy chrome blankets so far from the sun
Logic of the world robbing you of your boner
Let's start reading today about murder
As respite from the widespread fact
Between death and my head
Boner. When leaving Dakar you can cut
Through the Doldrums. Hugging
The equator with your unfertilizing
Wing. His sonata for the left hand went
Unplayed. I've been instructed to say
I'd rather not touch them. Today
Was supposed to change my life.
I sat around pouring my money
Into the pit. That was kind
Of calming. This is moving
Up. I consumed quietly my tasteless
Food. I stared devoutly into my
Phone in the capital city of the culture
Of the age. It was a somewhat spiritual
Serfdom for which we had all volunteered
But it did still feel kind of weird to acknowledge
In the David H Koch Dinosaur Wing
He who once stood upright with god
Knows what is in his hand

HE SMELLED ANDROGENIC

Gulls were screaming

Overhead & moaning

Foghorns like the manatees

Of sound made a canopy

Over whirring lawn

Mowers. His lower

Lip quivered. He

Was narrating his sex

History for me to make

The proposition clear

It was too clear

It was time to go

Shopping or do beauty

Things to ready

Myself for something

Like the reconciliation

Of empirical and spiritual

Truths at last in

Like real time

CHINOOK

I am so so loose and free
I am the imitation of everything

Wing of idiocy
Sun fattening against the sky

Picture the day
Beginning as a post

Unfurling as such
Into the truth...

I have stretched that word so far
Am I even a woman anymore

I have stretched my word so far
I no longer know its value

Something wet...
Stiffening the air

Like a sex breeze
And it passes

The houses against the pale blue which radiates
And which one evening was starred by the redness of bombs!

It could have been a poet in the Spanish
Civil War... It could be a Syrian

Poet or a Russian poet and a poet
From a country I don't know...

But it's Rimbaud... I was watching a movie... chickens
Were being killed... then geese...

Then chickens... the prayer

No that wasn't how it was
The outside... of your survival

The hide of your face
Its rugged pores

No she was a pert
Small woman with an Anna

Karenina face. No her
Face was an Anna Karina

Light your candles
Poetry fans

Go down
Go down

Go down into your bodies and pray there

SAINT JOHN PASSION

I found my earbuds & put them in
& turned on the *St John*

Passion. The conductor was a woman
From Oregon. I could see a woman

With warts out the corner of my eye
Across from me. Chewing energetically

The train was not moving. It was not going
To move. My pants tight and my shoes

Uncomfortable. Exactly two warts
On your face, chewing woman, pivoting

Now forty-five degrees to face me

ME TOO

he's   using his phone to choke
&   kill small animals

but   I... but I
wanted...

to   be free... she protested
she   was lying   cousin

of   explaining
Laura   Dern's hair

subway   in which not poems
but   the idea of poetry's been deployed

to   sell life insurance
a boring   but also morally

disquieting   thing to buy   intimating
the   entire orchestra

melting   asphalt in
Australia

you   *would* take it
seriously   a Barthes an anthropologist

would   but those days r over... you...
you   would... likewise

tune   it out   we would   we all work
so hard   smoking the steam

off   longing
more than anyone can spend

fried   sacred bird
Laura   Dern's hair

a   cooked
black   vein wheeling

into   the bulging bloodshot
eye   of the lotus   I'm keeping

this one   more truthful
more   sensual

a   room full of beautiful women in black
but   I too was an actor

nobody knew I was lying
I was that good

still   I can't abdicate the leadership
of this movement to actresses

see   how I dissemble in the dark
even now

to my very
organs   even to my owen

soul   Salvador Salvador
the surf   was stiff

like a Kennedy's
hair   I too carried

a device   like that
even hiding

from the world   to it
I was a king

good   reason to be combed
from   a thousand

apposite   but dead
causes

go   within my child
said   the parody of a guru

without me   single
sandaled

foot
in   snow

one   slender
foot in the door

MOM JEANS

In my torment I imagined myself speaking
I imagined myself having recourse to speech

Morning glories flickered up and down
On a chainlink fence. My arms were heavy

My tummy like a mummy. I'll just sit here
& let somebody who doesn't know me tell me

What to do with my body. I like this drawing
Of the girl with fangs. The air is bloated

It says DON'T TALK TO ME. The blood
In my veins swells my very hands

With reluctance to describe anything
Anything at all for you, like a dumb

Animal at a letterbox withdrawing
Her ticket. Just like a dumb animal

Withdrawing her ticket from circulation
In England in a closed children's book

With dented crayoned pages waiting
Inside a Salvation Army somewhere

That we're not going to go into today

THE CHLOROPHYLL IN HER WATER MATCHES

for Dana Greene

The chlorophyll in her water matches

The night vision light in *Collateral*

Murder. I'm in bed with a man

In Paris. He's a little "older"

Long curly hair and nice thick

Body, kind of an absent lover.

There are sliding glass doors

Mirrors around us so we can

See everything. I see my

Tentative movements which

I adjust to improve what

They implicate. I am

"Young and insecure."

We get dressed. I go

Back to "my" apartment

Where my roommate asks

Me what I want to do.

I say I still feel like fucking

But not the guy I just did

It with, knowing inwardly

I would do it with him again

But I left something soft

Of myself in that room

I won't make the mistake

Of bringing into the next one

I was always the enemy

Of my every softness

You might say I had

Learned it somewhere

You might speculate

Where. In sex it is

Possible to hide. You

Can hide in there forever

If you want. This

Is Paris my roommate

Says, it's like whatever

She flips her hair

She means nobody

Need interrogate me

On my desires or whether

They're real much less

Just. The part

Of them that's real

Is real. She opens

A big can of cannellini

And spills them over

Her right shoulder

Ritualistically. Little

White beans bounce

And roll around

Our cluttered room

DIARY

Well I'm alone today musing
Wrathfully on J's beauty
A hideous emphysemic cough
Keeps boiling up the airshaft
Somebody's blasting
The carnival music of her
Homeland. We have to do
What we can. I found half
A cat turd on my comforter
My boyfriend is a beautiful
Busboy. I'm trapped.

DOUBT

You asked about my doubt

I was afflicted with a normal amount of doubt

Which was an intolerable

Amount

WELLFLEET

it is such a silence that its gloss
would take forever

like a face whose sun is a con
like the veil warmed by this selfsame con
like seven veils each on the seven
gay pillars
rubbed down with creamsicles and attar
of rose

i mean
what i mean...
maybe i want to end it
what i mean is i want it razed

like a Z hissing thru white underpants
hot with spit... many
Zs...

and vermeil Zs from cartoon sleeps when your body says drugs
when the sun drops its goo down your vents
and the more you lick them the more the speakers hiss

and that's like... adulthood

when i pried open your ass
i smelled the fried chicken you'd eaten

or when our fuck was like a greek coin

and i yearned to fall down in worship

or how myrrh smells like shit

exactly

like sweet shit
on fire

is it active enough to be itself

he chortled... rubbed with herbs...

the sky was vapid and seething
all morning
i had no money
the entire quarter consumed
in such silence
its steps and the stoops of its steps
consumed
in such glacial
silence i knew it was the sound
of slowness
to which the air itself was palpably
even as we walked through it
capitulating

just a ripple
shaking down its pole...

when the belly really is the middle
it has its own navel

your belly
softening under its navel

the sun whitening down from the stars that tickle
a spider's legs into the anxiety
which becomes her murder her absolute
form... i mean

this state

i was born in it...

and having returned to it can only think
the only thing that makes any sense

is to have come out of it never to return

...

here is a ticket
it is an ancient ticket

it is about fifty years old

do you think it's still good
it depends
when snow blankets the pass

our days spun to particles that shine
even when we hate them... just like everyone else's

like this extreme
fineness

did not just happen...

it was made

by an asshole who took

and it

is like
freedom

it is like freedom sometimes...

it is so big...

too big
not to be grand...

but it is not grand...
but it is so big

...

this embraced you
from all sides
like the gelid
god it was
with
its zapping clitoral elves by the hundred ten
hundred billion thousands in a hiss of clean soda water

accomplishing turnings acclaimable feats tricking on the dusky loom of Kabir
means-wrought ends achieved in absolute
butts and total finishes that bury your face in blooms
gushing dickhole tears that once you've dealt them
you've smelt them and once you've done that it's like
you took their smell away

but you didn't mean to

you're a nice person
like...

when it's too raw to be free
but that's freedom

when uvular clots spewing yogurt and minerals
in a sea of boiled wool
still has a winner
even though it sounds equal
just because it sounds equal
it still has a winner
and its winner
is me

i mean when like

you're sucking

the pit of the peach
until your tongue is sore
until your tongue is tonsured
until you've swallowed your tonsured tongue
swallowed

beowulfs... maccabees...

the trick that the moon is small...

like why don't you get
that it's only a trick

that the moon is small...

actual men... near like the moon
are there any
the moon is hung
at the end of a dark arm
over us a warm arm
our arm
and it from where we are is equal
to the sun and it does matter
where we are
it matters where we are

it puts a cloud of ink in my jelly
in the dew-gels now everywhere cropping up on the shoals

it runs like razors along the sides of a school

of fish slicing your forelegs open in the sea which is
not a sea but the ocean...

at its outermost

where the lords
which are only shoulders athwart heads all bemossed and in concert
turn toward the edge where the sun dips
under...
which under
when it's hard to swallow
the seat
of the first end
to a day where the throat

closes and gags
on the sun

mountains unbegrimed but submerged but
still
retaining their heads

when
the sun dips
below the row at the outermost lip
of the world

and when the copper-colored humped
back of the part
of the universe we can see from there
obviously
copulating with its other
unseen regions that it obscures with its heaving
when the copper-colored humped
back of the part
of the universe we can see from there
uncoils
like the thing that shot pain into your friend's head when he thought it
    was love
he was making and that was his
load he was going to get to be blowing
when the copper-colored humped back of this
side of the copulating universe uncoils
and unbends and sighs its very long
milk sighs of years

by the hundred thousand millions eddying into pools
at the edge of the eye of the lucky one
when its ducts are sucked for the buds that hurt when they give

the sky
the blue line drawn
at the top of the page by the four-year-old
the blue line drawn by the boy
representing the sky

might be seen
for once

to be where it is: also
under us

TIFFANY'S POEMS

Love is irreversible
Versible
Versible
—Mary J. Blige

SIC

Roses are red
Pirates are booty
Your name is Tiffany
Kalamooty

I have to get it all down Tiffany
Everything I can recollect from our first night
Before we meet again & the world convulses

I should have written immediately
But I was out of money
Then I got paid & it wasn't enough
I'm not making excuses
For failing to write when happy
Nor for the mechanism of pennilessness
Which like a high-tech athletic garment
Wicks all moisture away from the body
& sucks up as thru an astral straw the subtle ointments
Of the pussy and in the name of Holy Secrecy
And in the name of THE LAW I had better write it all down today
While my computer's still dead & the phone
I forgot at home's still at home with you in it
Wait for me
Like a slender girl in an old Chinese poem
When we were fucking on the bathroom floor Tiffany
On the night of the Sad Party
Tiffany Absence From God
Tiffany Absolute Liberty

DREAM

I dove under water
Under salt water
Ocean water
While a party continued upon the surface
It was night
Lights danced upon the waves
Diving to the bottom at night
"Some are born to endless night"

And a voice came
And a voice said

MAGNIFY MY EYE
MAGNIFY MY EYE
MAGNIFY MY SURFACES'
CAPACITY
FOR BEAUTY

SCRAMBLED EGGS

for Dana Ward

Once upon a time

There was a carriage

Ahead of the woman pushing it

As other carriages before that

One were preceded by horses

Perambulator's the long

Word for pram. I learned

"Pram" from Mary Poppins

The movie. "Dear

If You Change" is a song

By John Dowland. Dear

If you change

But you have

As the wavering

Document amounts

Only to my constancy

I didn't have the money but bought

A shirt cos I had it in mind

To please her for whom

I have yet to wear it

A beauty

Of tiny and devastating

Accuracies incidentally

I keep on taking a pill

It sickens me

Blots

With fecal cloths

My sun

Blots with doom muslins

With dread rags

My face whose small sabbath face

In any case can't be seen

When the chemicals of displeasure boil up

From the base as the bad burlesque

Of pleasure

& the Darth Vader of horniness

Like a horn being torn

From the face whose tears

I would one by one collect

For you in a blotter if I could trust

You and/or you and your heart's

Blotter as the dead composer's

Emotions are entrusted to the music

In which they are preserved

A bright machine he made for the worlds

That he felt

Within him

Only

Preserve me

From shame when I play

Upon my strings in the secret ships

In whose locks I repeat the hurts

And melodies one cherishes best

Alone in the dark

SHE HELD

onto me after she came

It's kind of ridiculous down there she said

Tiffany
Has on white cotton Calvins which her pussy has soaked
Tiffany is holding onto me
Then I let two tears jump out of my eyes

Tiffany frics mc a sausage and a
egg

She serves them with sprouts & excellent
mustard & tea

Please do tell me more about Persia
Its thick black hair is crowned underneath
By a very small mouth

It was a happiness
What do you want from me
It was a happiness
I recalled trying to imagine planning a novel but what
If I was trying to forget
What if I was trying to be the best
Forthwith I banished all literary sensations
Which is why this book isn't any good

TIFFANY MADE ME

        squirt
I cried
And now I'm losing
Now I know I'm going to lose

LAMBADA LITERARY AWARD

Color of Star Wars
There were boxlike wooden stairs
Under the water
The places where one can be pulled under
A woman took my hand
Not to have written is to resign oneself to oblivion on the one hand
But on the other it is to turn oneself over
To liberty
For once
For one does forget how to do it
One forgets having ever known how
Then more leaves blow onto the sea & it ends

THE THOUGHT "THE GREATEST CITY IN THE WORLD"

was englobed by my skull as the train pulled away
trains projects cars Greece
clouds the houses have roofs
I have learned so many forms
[of sorrow.] Of sorrow I could say
in a different room
& of poesy in my day

Imagine having a place in society
And love
This is it
This is the lordly wonder
What makes my mouth water
To see this world
To be of *this* world & no other
To know a few of its customs
I was thinking about learning to paint
Although I have no talent for it
And no leisure time
But I did photograph a pale blue mosque-like dome for Tiffany
& she wrote me something in Arabic
It looks beautiful and I can't understand it
& I shouldn't but I look beautiful too

IT LOOKS BEAUTIFUL AND I CAN'T
UNDERSTAND IT SAID GOD

Spirits can and do fall
Moisturized air of bread baking
It is so hard to chronicle the news
The feeling when my phone doesn't work
That everyone I love likes me a little
Less
It is hard to withstand the love of one I cannot reciprocate
It is also hard to bear the love I feel but cannot because neither can she admit
It's been twenty-four hours or so since I last saw T
I felt rather stupid in too-heavy shoes
But something had to hold me down
The Ecstasy of Communication is a book by Jean Baudrillard I have been
      experiencing as a feeling
But now my pill is dispersing its evil throughout me
& now M sends a picture of his dick, long & straight-like & like a T-square
Perpendicular
To his paint-spattered shorts
& I am alone
With my job

ALL DEAD

The saint ascending to fill her raiment of cloud
Robes velvet bouffants great gobbets and crowns all misted with salt rinds
A bellows a boy's cheeks a boy's birthday wish
All of them stopped up in my palsied hand
All dead unblown by my brass instrument

THE STORES ARE FULL

Could it be Tiffany of attractive and charming objects
For a noble and hardworking people
Who rise for love and shun war
Who are all as good as we are

IF THESE POEMS WERE TIFFANY'S

That is if she took them
As she has
Less often than I take her
Taken me
I should be reading Orlando Furioso
I could declaim only as Orlando Furioso
While eating all the costly medicinal foods they sell in my dying city
And then I'd finally be a poet
Perpendicular to the ages
But I don't think she will

SHE

wants something not "i don't have" but can't give
is it
my body
no
it's the desire in it
the desire is real
and i can't give it
i give all the rest of what there is
but how does *that* come out of me
my desire
that's mine
yet it does pour from me
it pours from me in waters and it pours from me
as tears
and i cannot give it
and i can never give it

25 AUGUST

I'm in new clothes, my old bad skin
Is clean. I worried the wen
On my jaw this morning, walking
Away from Tiffany's. My period
Started in American Apparel Outlet
I know I've irretrievably ruined something
Hello, a tall girl in high jeans &
Perfect clogs kept saying. I could tell
She was sweeter than her faultless
Bangs suggested. Nauseating
Purchase. But it's the stout I mean the start
Of the school year and I have this job. Give
Me courage. Keep
Me scrappy. The blood is descending
Me. It is doing the surge
Downward and it is doing the red death
Flume screaming Tiffany where its boar
Is wrapped around my tooth and where
It is smelling Tiffany. I am alone. Where
Isis is still just a song
By Bob Dylan & where the hottest places
Are still only as hot as once they were. You tried
Hard to survive. And for what. For this
Possibly for this. What Sunder said: *I couldn't fall*
Asleep until I could think a thought
That would make me smile. I'd been crying
All night. But finally I remembered
That John Philip Sousa wrote an opera
Called THE GLASS BLOWERS.
And then I fell asleep.

UNANSWERED QUESTION

I'd like to account for some of the things I've done, I feel
It would save me from oblivion, if only in this moment,
With "The Unanswered Question" in my ears. I've just
Given $100 to Dave—$80 to return to Mom,
Who loaned me that many dollars last Monday,
And $20 for them to spend on food. Yesterday
She broke her arm. She called me in the morning.
"You're not going to like this..." and proceeded to
Demand that I get an orthopedic surgeon to come to
Her. I wish I could have. Inwardly I accused myself
For not having become one. I called Montefiore, her second-
Choice hospital, then 911. Then I met Tiffany
And her friends at Home Depot and pretended
They were my family. Tiffany's leg
Against mine in the Iranian restaurant.
Tiffany's eyes. Tiffany saying, in front
Of her friends, "The smooth bottom
Of Ariana." When Tiffany puts small kisses upon you
When she fucks you at the African burial ground
On September Eleventh and then, perhaps a little rudely
And perhaps a little obviously
Sneers *That was for YOU*

HOW COME

I remember

"Tam-o'-shanter"

Is it because my great-

Grandmother was a milliner

The point is I saw a woman

Exit a clinic wearing a coral-

Colored one large enough

For some medieval tapestry

Tiffany

Are you home yet

THE LONG LOVE THAT IN MY THOUGHT DOTH HARBOR

I saw a gorgon on the cover of SPORTS ILLUSTRATED

She wore a metal dress

Her condition had been caused, it said, by her hunger

I saw a cactus like a chorister and one like a church deacon

And many small stones and growing things like sea urchins, all spines

I saw the best minds

I saw the best minds

I saw the best minds

I texted that I had the impression I'd left a burning building

I texted that I'd read FAST COMPANY cover to cover

I read that George and Amal were splitsville

I told no one

I bled through my cutoffs on my way to SAFEWAY

I stole a SAMBAZON green juice and collected $75 via WESTERN
    UNION at Customer Service

It happened four times that a man hung his head out the window of his
truck to bark at me woof woof

Once it sounded like hoochie hoochie

I don't know I can't see myself

I never make eye contact

I can see myself

I am a mummy

Walking along the road

The mummy of my thoughts

Whereas she had now become the very mummy of her thoughts wrote the
female George Gordon Lord Byron in my mind

Walking down the road thinking HOROWITZ IN MOSCOW

Walking down the road thinking SANTIAGO DE COMPOSTELA

Walking down the road thinking THE LIVING ROAD

Walking down the road thinking THE ROAD

I entered OFFICEMAX and purchased there for more than a dollar a
SNICKERS, my breakfast

I entered AXIS MART and purchased there for fifty-seven cents a bag of
   sunflower seeds, my brunch

Walking down the road I brought out from my pocket what felt like a
   flattened chocolate wrapped in foil

It was an off-white stone in the shape of a tooth

A line was circling

It was a line like

When our skulls were begging bowls

Or

When our skulls were mortars

I was thinking I wasn't ever going to have the mind to write it

I was thinking I wasn't ever today going to have the mind to write it

When I ground dry pink peppercorns into my ears like birds

The sound of birds was also in my ears

And now that you are grasping the small warm body gently between
   thumb and forefinger

And Venus is wearing a helmet

And I'm bleeding all over her iron dick

No that's not it

Or Mars is wearing a red dress and piano keys and gladiolas and Lorcas are
lynching themselves all over the yellow cactus flowers

Are we there yet are we there yet are we there yet

No

Her white fingers gathered up from the table its slender crusts

The Cold War was over its broad white lines

The Civil War was over Scarlett O'Hara fluttering her hundreds of white
tablecloths in surrender

It really exhausts me how the country won't remember or what men are

Or what exhausts me is the thought that revolves into the thought of a
wanderer

Which is the thought of an escapee

Which is the thought of one who cannot have a thought

Which is the thought of one who has none

Mother Russia seeping red into my antiqued American head

All the JUVÉDERMs on the long honey-blonde hairs of HERMITAGEs
and glasswares

Mother Russia stalking like the panther of Josephine Baker across the very
broad desert of my empty begging bowl

Mother Russia purring like an idling ROLLS-ROYCE or like the leopards
of Haile Selassie

And she is there revolving like the faded TASMANIAN DEVIL tattoos of
this world

She is there revolving like all things that revolve in the mind like TAZ

Revolving in me *like ancient women gathering fuel in vacant lots*

Do you remember when FIRE & ICE was a bad perfume

Or when the Cold War divided the world into chess and space

Do you remember when space was a race

Or when god gave us race as a toy to delight us, as once

I thought in the only glee of your bed, or else

We misremember

I remember when I misread on a road sign SCRIABIN

If I do not become a corporation I will never beat the assholes to the moon

If someone is to go to the moon let me sing you a love song

Let it be me

I emptied my dark DIVA CUP onto the splendid kirtle of Venus

During the snows of the last three weeks in New York City I attempted a short-
   circuit study of the use of lead pipe in the plumbing of Imperial Rome

Down into myself today near high noon I poured what I had stolen, not a
   fine juice but one reconstituted from powder

Which like a double phoenix with the SNICKERS and the seeds of the
   flowers of the sun and the self-sloughing uterine wall within me began
   to revolve

Like a DESERT STORM and like old bad sensations from the stressful
   children's game OPERATION

And like the idiot fume I spray on you with all the cut-glass champagne-
   colored atomizers I stole from Frank O'Hara poems

And now that we are whirling slowly

Eating our emeralds

Revolving in all we do not know and all we have forgotten

And now that we are wearing our melancholily slanted hats

And bleeding remembering all the mistrals that have never blown into
our faces

And all the poems that we have never read and the adolescent brown
fingers of the bright boy we never were and the sense of meat loaf
being finally what the guts make from whosoever we have failed to
disperse into English

Now that we are revolving one like the other my dear

And gradually I am attaining again my customary cadence

—after that it cuts off.

21 february 2015

NINE MOONS

Apparently I have a body that produces a lot of blood
You have to let me take your picture if you pour your blood on the sand
    you said
I guess I did. I remember being in love with you & I remember
Learning to like you & I remember that the vigilance of justice
Like an idea in my furnace
Is never so clear as the times in my life I've truly truly lived as one enthralled.

It seems to me every person
Wants a heart beating
At the root of the rightness
Of things

Or else we misremember

The difference between the idea of possession
& everything else in the whole wide world

In other words every person is already in possession of what
If she could only speak she might not so much proclaim but know
As that beyond all aspiring which nevertheless is the only
Thing

But now it is making me do my didactic thing

Mists dissolving into the calves & shoes of the mind
The shoulders of the prurient young sisters & the money so coyly
Disdaining total hiddenness among the teeth of a certain
Man's smile

A truth so free
& so easily misbegotten its clauses cannot close. A truth
Like the fat moon bursting over these mountains called Organ
Which in the old days in Spanish I hear were called Oblivion

A truth so free you too are unworthy of it, one
Even whose shadow I risk deforming in this secret place
So many have worked so long & hard to make safe for delicate things.

"Things."

I said it again.

At White Sands yesterday my skin was browner
Than it now seems & my heart was lighter
Lighter, you might say, than it deserves
& a fine sheet of black rain covered
The fulminating ochre slot I watched opening in the clouds
Thru which we could all at once perceive the sun
Waning like the fires in an old black oven. One made of iron.

& yesterday

We saw a rainbow

& during the three days preceding yesterday we saw two

& surely at least that makes seven kinds of good omen
Multiplied by three in the infinite styles of light that made me
Also think without paying it too much mind yesterday
That now I'd really have to reread the part in the Bible about the arc
That follows the Flood, after the raven
& after the dove, but like so many books that are closed in my mind in
    the end
I left this one closed too, the way I found it. Instead I let the seven
    porticoes
Of everyday light like the jewel that time itself declined
Loll open inside my little mind. Loll open like a thing perhaps
But just slightly better than any secondhand thing
Like perhaps a certain implement
From an old, neglected sacrament
Like a thing in the mind
A thing in *my* mind
Or more
Like you, my love,
Like you

5 may 2015

NINE
NEOCLASSICAL
POEMS

He said, If I answer your question, are you going to say something bad
about me.
He said, If I tell you, what are you going to say about me.

ALCIBIADES

A few months ago my mother told me my father raped her

When things came to a head

Alcibiades broke the dicks off the herms

Deserted Athens

Went over to the Spartan side

Of the world

My mother says many untrue things

I keep going

Around the world breaking

Something in

My memory, at the flare

In my root but it won't go away

LIKE TWO EMPTY WALLETS MY BOOBS

Like two empty wallets my boobs

Flank my heart in readiness

For you, LORD, you

For you, LORD, you. For

You, LORD, you

For you

For you

For you who no

Longer

Enrapture us

CRYSTAL GEYSER

I was looking for a woman

To bury my darkness in

That's her blood on my dick

Our drapes fell

Like night curtains fluttering

Their empty sleeves prolapsed

Into the dream

In which I kept my eye fixed

On a delight beyond all picturing

I kept my head; the word

Retrieved from a mountain

Sprouting like hairs upon a sage

I was supposed to remember

I'm supposed to know what I think

Lingering over the regrets in my instrument

Love clapped, grooves soaked in tongues

Iron sheets

Fer dans nôtre coeur

For the night my child hath two pillars: twin invoices

Two rogues, two roes

That are twins. Between rigor

And mercy's the invisible door

In the meantime consider this jar

Of standing gray water, Englishy, invisibly brooding

This larval anecdotal jar

I've tied

Around my neck with a string so it bangs

As I walk against my rectangular heart

PROMETHEUS OR SOMETHING

something strange, something physical, gravel rattling over a burning
     plate in the belly, corrosive dread like frothing and seething, a fecal
     feeling, a dead feeling.

gray paste, gray wastes, gray clay filling up the places where guts & light
     used to be.

the sensation of shame, physical substance, germinated low flame at
     the bottom of my organs growing day by day into a secret sheath of
     redness, battery acid dissolving my insides.

stupefaction in mind & limbs, exhausted arms & jellied, boneless legs,
     burned by the flare at the center that was always hot in a very bad
     way but gave no energy or joy.

like the word frigid, the word rigid, becoming a canopic jar for the
     organs of a dead thing, aura wizening, drying out, and breath by
     breath being sucked back into the body, of the body becoming the
     stiffening mummy of a very bad secret, painfully preserved, chained
     to the rape rock, skin hanging off her like a ghost, you're inside the
     jar and you are a jar, worry doll stuffed with stones.

I'D LIKE

To have an experience

Of myself

As more

Columnar

Guess

That's why I came here

Standing

Up, standing up for myself

Or else flying

Into evening digs

The pit

In the gut.

To be like god put on

A stone face. I could

Use an injection

I could talk

Thru the stiff

Polymers

Like so many

Persimmons

Sweating

Against the jade Buddha

Buttering, creaming

The last of my redness

Surgically

Removed

Small words

In faces of putty & bone daring

You to accuse them

Of not having

Hearts

DITCH FACE

Kris Jenner kind of has ditch face

I had it too when I ate the most

Pills, like, the face I hung

Over smooth brown thighs

& hid behind my hair

Who will be honest about the terrible sadness

Of worlds condemned to the scroll

I was waiting for you

To do it but you never

Did

Ancient ticker

Rock face

Rubbery fuck hole

Getting old

Yea the beasts do groan

Massaged into my hair, lit up by my numerals

Let me not forget

My lord and let me not forgive

Let me not forget O lord when I go down

To the bottom of the Nile like old

Lady arms whistling in the breeze let me not

Forget O lord

What I went down there to do

RIGID FRIGID BE WITH ME SAINT BRIGID

I hugged my mother
Now I smell of her

When you and I were pretending
To sleep alongside each other

Your heartbeat
Rocking the bed, your dick

Heavy in the small
Of my back

Until at last like a choked
Flame it guttered

& went out

Too much bad still buried in my body
For me to let anyone in

Sent via BlackBerry from T-Mobile

awoke nothingness was seething

All around me like a soda & the black

And vapid heat was bleating, pealing in a ring

Around my head. The head that had forsaken

Its matter and seen fit to become the brute

That could learn to survive anything, anything.

While I was upright

I mean away

While I was doing my job

My man

Fell apart. It was sixty-

Four degrees at eleven pm

In New York City and it was boring

Being a good person on the fourteenth

Of December

Two thousand fifteen

THE WAR ON APRIL

for Geoffrey G. O'Brien

This is the song that doesn't end

Bright with riches

White with remorse

Vitiating your demises muffining

Them into the breakfasts that churn

On the vitamin-fat tongue of the swallower

So the sun pours down its liquor

To redden my greenish

White thighs as my father's

Beard is spangled with raspberry

Buds, little blood bladders, for he's

Demolishing a turnover in the ripening

Melon of my wee memowwy

Where he also is dying.

For I know not he. Absolving

Brains. Smashing pumpkins, bags

Of Bugles, bags of nineteen sixties

Balloons on pegs in holes on squares

Of yellowing foamcore where I leave

Me now to languish over your

Canadian bacon–like cheek. It's a wet

Brown dick & it's chirping like a bird.

I spit on it, wow, amazing

Like oil-mussed gulls

Downily flitting expiring on a tire iron

Half exposed in the sand which

Too is wet & fretful

This is the song that doesn't end.

First I put on my helmet

Then I took it off.

Owning everything

I did not possess I said Son

Of Sam like a stripper's

Blister oozing undetected

Within her mule's

Embrace. Golden dogs

Were trotting. Armaments

Of the jolly. I died

Before I ever remembered

To make the document

Called Jolie-laide. Was it

Because I got too busy "just

Being a woman" for once I mean

Delivering myself

Like a dresser

Drawer offering

Herself up to the stoutness

Of her camarade, tidy

& full of the things of his beauty

He said yes a little too easily

But ok I'll say yes to you too

Singed broccoli florets of my heart

Burnt caramels, as though I cared

For foreign words

In italics, I do not

Or for engines, bruises

Turning colors rifling the docs

None shall open. But a horsey

Wind down from the Alps

Will one day come to comb

Back their hair

& whisper vile things

In their unhearing ear

Without the brains behind

These muzzles ever knowing

Anything about it. For they eat only

The weeds that they behead.

Go to your room.

ROTISSERIE

Took me an hour kissing to wash

The ashes out of your mouth

Eat things

That's how you make them go away

That's what these people here are doing

Things go inside them to die or dead

Things go in them to live

I was lying awake next to you thinking

About being a woman falling far

Below standard

I was lying awake paying strict attention

To the boring feeling of not deserving to live

It took so long I

Read three pieces of penetrating internet

Journalism, "related" to them

The way seeing anything at all

Is a kind of commendation

Verging dangerously upon acclaim

Just seeing

Simply having seen

Then like a father I

Turned away from you

& delivered my head to the suctioning

Action of my device

My recollections having already been composed

By it for me I just turned rotisserie

Pink on the spit of my & everybody else's

Good intentions & that was the day

No it had already happened a billion

Times no that WAS the day the music

Died

BITCH OF THE WORLD

Alone and so insane
My muscles on fire
My skin on fire
I will fucking die nothing meaningless

The bilge my heart pumping
Thru itself & thru me while I'm drowning
In feeling that does not even belong to me
The same bilge thru which you are scrolling
And scrolling in the holy, old way

I was once a searcher
Among the chaff, a poet with one eye
Always open for things that glimmer
Now I'm just another pipe fitting
On the imperial plumbing
Thru which the culture flushes its waste

I KNOW FROM EXPERIENCE IF THE DIFFICULT POEM

for Charity Coleman

I know from experience if the difficult poem

Is not completed in the moment the courage

And occasion are unlikely to meet me together

For its sake again. It will be a new elocution

I still won't have been able to face the truth enough

To meet that I'm evading next time I fail to face

Myself, next time I'm just too scared.

I miss a sweetness. I miss

Winter & the sadness of winter, swelling

Through the fruits rotting in my motherless

Womb. Charity

Gentle bravery, take it

From me, a woman bad at trying, take

From me the pain of similarity in the sweetness

Of gratitude burned to a crisp in the scintillae

In what's left of my slender

Goodness

FOLK SONG

I lack the courage

(she said)

To show my pain

For fear it would twist

Into the burlesque of itself

& turn around (she continued) to throttle

Me the second

I get it out. Therefore (she, she averred)

I have no choice

But to claim the exuberance of Picasso

Preserved here (she gestured) among these lesser-

Known sculptures now

On view in the Museum of Modern Art.

Finding in any case no vigor left

In the dominant mode of the day's laments

(She went on) and moreover bored

With all of them

I'll just turn gray enough

To merge with the horizon, where all the Archaic

Smiles of all the old ejaculating

Ages go on shooting

The same dull white secrets into my transparent mouth

ON THE NIGHT OF TIFFANY'S THIRTIETH BIRTHDAY

There was a row of dark-

Eyed women, there were two

Rows of them at a table in the front

Room of Spain & every one

Of them was strange & every last

One of them was beautiful

It was a world far away

Full of ideas blessedly

Superior to those of my culture & these were some

Of its women. It was the twenty-first

Of December two thousand fifteen.

They were divining

The future from a green book

Of Hafez & a woman named Scheher-

Azade, I mean Shahrzad

With laughing eyes & witty smile told mine

Right out of the poem.

It said if I don't like my lot

In life I should consider the fact

I never tried for it, that trying

Might be a good idea, that now

Was a good time to start.

The second instruction

More of a statement really

Was that the love being offered me

Was real

TIKKUN OLAM

all those years i hid behind my veil
like an old god at last mature enough to know his own ugliness
yet so impressed with the transubstantiation of his pain

at no one's prompting
at no one's bidding
with the encouragement of no one
suddenly he longs to reveal himself to you
whom he made

but could not prepare himself for the sudden awe and shame
when he first recognized himself in you
then sensed, grimly, darkly, that something beyond him was streaming
    through you
something from higher
something from further away
a light from beyond
him, from before he knew himself to be
now rending him everywhere with a longing
to find out his own origins

IF I WON IT THEN I WON IT ONLY

If I won it
Then I won it only
By a word

I only won
It if I won it
By a word
By a word

I scarcely understood

If I won it
Then I won it
Only
By a word

By a word

I only won it
If I won it
By a word
By a word

By a word

I GOT USED

Sun in the sky
Gold in the ground

I got used
To all this misspent wealth

Sun in the sky
Gold in the ground

I'm just, I was only, I was only listening for a hum

On the line between the words as they space out

Listening for something dispirited

& enchained that you're hiding
I know it behind
Your every pleasant word

If I keep talking to you like this

Sun in the sky
Gold in the ground

If I keep letting you talk to me like this

Sun in the sky
Gold in the ground

You're going to force me to be a person
I know it

You're going to turn me into the kind of person
You're becoming. I can feel it

If I answer you

ALL I HAVE TO DO

Is look at you

To know. I can see every ejaculation
That's come from you in want

Of company hanging in the air
Around your head like a dingy veil

My heart makes a small movement
Toward your predicament while other parts

Within me turn away. How could someone so beautiful
Be so alone. How could someone so beautiful be so alone.

Apparently God wants us all revolving
Around the same question, his problem, as though

That could make us forgive him and maybe it could
The jealousy and spite and rage and lust his loneliness

First loosed upon the world
The harder thing than forgiving

Would be desiring
You whom I now pity

You whose secrets of taking my breath
Away are now arrayed

Around your sad halo like so
Many rusted tools

My genital hardens and rises and flops back
Upon its belly again, almost believing that awe

And forgiveness could physically both sigh
Out of a single breath while another eye

Inside my eye turns away
From you & back into the hammered copper

Blackness within myself where it pools
And foams into a velvet upon which

My heart rocks backward
Like a warm rock

Falling back and back and back
Onto the ground where anyway it came from

STILL GROANING UNDER ALL SHE OWED

Still groaning under all she owed to men
She turned toward the wider world
Where loathing was trumping
Love to great acclaim. Where nothing
Possessed vitality but loathing
The wind beneath the wings of Satan
Whipped by the silly putty Pegasuses
Of the snarling enormous Satan
Whipping her stupefied head till
She bowed down
Exhausted. Whose mind
Are you for? I'm sick
Of these colors she answered. So
They did the only kind thing.
They took out her eyes

NINE NEOCLASSICAL POEMS

I was thinking about my problems
PILLARS OF THE STATE I thought &
Then
BORROWED
WOOD
I thought Dawn Lundy Martin
"IF WE COULD DO WITHOUT
HIM WE WOULD"
Then my father arrived, no
But we weren't
Talking but into my mind he
Came. Then came THE UNIVERSAL SOLVENT
Harry Houdini was buried
Close to me
He is not
Buried
Close to where I am buried
He is
Buried
Close to where I live
In chains
Old marble sweating like soap
Under the cypresses under
The cypress trees.
Under
The sun
A redhead or a
Roadside

Candle
MINISTRY OF PUBLIC
WORKS
The card
From MONOPOLY the card in it
Called WATERWORKS
Universal solvent
The water of Flint
The spine inside her house that read
PUBLIC SMILES PRIVATE TEARS
Was a paperback your mother's mother
Read. TORN LACE
CURTAIN. Another one
Of hers
She liked those
Things. Sensations. Interiors
In Flint
In private
Hiring a private
Dick. Hiring
Him when she has
To. If.
When the law
Is unjust
Turning
On the
Lightswitch
Reading her

What she likes.
Doing
That
Very very very
Very slowly. Black grass
On my black
Beard
I'm picking thru
I'll go
Picking
Thru this
Mess
I am faithful
To my wife still
Soaping
Soaping your hand now very
Very
Very very very very very very
Quietly

FKN ZIGGURATS

for Julian Talamantez Brolaski

Not known are the things that will do God
—Egyptian Book of the Dead

FKN ZIGGURATS

My thighs r so stacked
Steep steep steep
Fkn ziggurats
4 u

IT IS A SUCKLING LOVE

It is a suckling love but
Large a stripling life
Touchless car
Wash and yet it and yet
And yet it makes
You glow n calluses
On yr fingers now
Rasping wordlessly thru me

DEMOCRACY NOW

A ratlike rodent went extinct today
I can't think
My thighs r so stacked
Fkn ziggurats
Soy no soy
Peanut no peanut
Very deep dimples
Hot cellulite light
Bleeding hard thru
Its panties 4 u

RAPES EONS FISHERIES

Rapes eons fisheries
Whipped waters lashes
Upon the back staved muscles
Starved engrovelated bones the fuck
Alloys the clams n oysters
The fucking shoals stripped
Bare of their muscles I do
Want you does that mean
I have to marry both coasts
All the veins in my arms stand
Up hard n blue little fingers
All over my screen little cells
Sighing little cells dying

YOUR POEM

Did I see the word LOVETINES
Or was that LOVELINESS
Furred ear of sleep, finches
At their labors, dragonfly
Purpose undisclosed to me
At the temple the tombeau
Of Paul Valéry

I CAN'T EAT YOU CAN'T SLEEP

Consumed with voluptuous privacy
My boat she sailed upon the surge
Fat bees come around me to suck
The flowers I cross my legs
Tight n hold in my nectar neither
Known nor seen do I want to be
Not even touched by none
But you but out the corner
Of my better eye I suppose I do
See shimmering the singed edges
Of my mortality the leaves of even
This book a breeze shall blow
Open the sun upon my shoulder
Where I cannot see it grazing
My secret forge the single
Yolk of an egg only the mouth
Of one poet

WHO AREN'T WE

It is a suckling life but large
Tho it b only suckling it b large
Memory the rasp within me iron tongs
Old andirons New England things
A taste of ash an old prosthetic
Limb unmourned soldiers from even
Older wars a thong still battening
Down the font at my navel to ye
Olde center of the Earth the haggard pits
Of presence & absence the selfsame
Dichotomy of the ages, eons of poetry
Descending on me now as simple froth
Like the brief career of that girl's latte
Art I mean where haven't I been who
Aren't I I mean where haven't we
Been who aren't we

PILGRIMS' PROGRESS

In SAFEWAY I heard a whining
Song. Dill filled the air with longing

What was the Twentieth Century
Appetite. I grew up wondering would I

Ever fuck like them, the dead. They left
Behind the lingering sense of an ethos

To discover love, if you could, in your
Own way for your own self, outside the dread

And shame they (the other they)'d installed all around you
Is the asshole closer to death, is shit close to it

And why when some pray do we put our ass
In the air to kiss the ground, the rosebud

Of the dark side of our minds waving in the blue
Sex and death got married and had a baby

I wasn't there when it happened and nobody exactly
Told me about it. There was a lingering scent on the air

My first years in New York going to the one no two really
Good nightclubs, when the Meatpacking District

Was still full of actual meat and blood and tall whores
In beautiful crowds picking carefully over the cobblestones

In their enormous heels and wigs. Here ends the only
Nostalgia I shall permit myself. I was feeling kind

Of Auschwitzy in a vegan restaurant in Warsaw.
There was an H&M and a multiplex across the street

From the ghetto wall nestled inside an apartment
Complex. I'm alive only because the false identity

My grandmother's husband bought her before he was killed
Meant she had a job just outside that wall. The malls

Are built all over the world that we might shop our way out
Of oblivion. It was easy to weep at the wall. I put

My forehead on it and said my dead uncles' names and Tadeusz
Richter the name of the man my grandmother actually loved.

A plague. A genocide. The usage of the world. Lathe
Of all difference. I used to have a nightmare that recurred

A spiral of water draining down a hundred thousand family
Pictures. None of them people I knew, all of them faces

I could love if I had the chance. The idea of loving as a public
Act is something I inherited. The felicity of men who fuck

Like friends is something I admire. The Emma
Goldman brilliancy and courage of the women

Of ACT UP! & Gran Fury, my living moral referent. But I
Don't know how to write a poem about AIDS.

I don't know anybody who died of it. I read Tim
Dlugos to face Warsaw because of a line about his

Father or grandfather speaking Polish. Can everything
Be made to resolve into *my* originary pain? What drove

My mother insane. And an idea of liberty and elegance
Perfected by gay men in cities: the constellation of my youngest

Desires. I'm on a banquette in Winslow Arizona next to my
Post-gender lover, my person. My dream of a Gay

Priesthood, queerness as a Kohanim, priest
Class of the world, with whom you get high, tend to the sick

And imprisoned, advocate for the misunderstood, and die
In grace. Where would we be without nightclubs, the liberation

Of sex from "love" as defined by heterosexist patriarchy, the lesbians
Who teach poetry in prisons, the women who radiate zero

Sexuality in order, like running fleeing nymphs to flee the frankly
Real male gaze, where would we be? Where would we be without

Chelsea Manning's agony? The Danse Macabre of plaguetime Paris?
The New York I never knew?

OPEN FIFTHS

I just watched a Tony Robbins video
You may judge this a counterrevolutionary gesture
Thinking about the people I forgot to write back to
I ate as much peanut butter as I could
Listening to I CAN'T HELP FALLING IN LOVE WITH YOU

(Pats the boot of his gun affectionately) a kind of bug
As siphoner sucking up the purple world thru its straw
Whorling hurricanes out from the backs of beetles, diaper rashes
Heavy tits heavy eyes of a heavy lady, a lady with fibroids
A lady who suffers migraines, I wanna fuck a woman who knows pain

I wanna feel the heat of a woman who knows pain
Yazidi women and girls call each other comrade
I'm not at all certain this is true
I met Pussy Riot at Richard Hell's one night, proceeded to not write about it
Richard had just read a thing in public to make him look like no friend
    to women

Then Pussy Riot called him wanting to be friends   the lord moves in
    mysterious ways
Richard's apartment is tiny it was an intimate affair   whiskey
And thick stew Sheelagh made   someone
Gave someone a suboxone. Nadya had a bad
Cold and a toothache. Maria though perhaps slightly less photogenic was
    sexier in person

I worship poetry she told me   what would I be if I came from such a country
Putin barechested on his horse & out a-raping
The people of Pushkin having not yet forgotten at which altar
To kneel & worship & I've run out of money
Again   there's really no excuse this time

The worship of certain maladaptive behaviors
As though they pertained to art but they do
In general it's my womanhood that takes the hit
I used to think the defining characteristic of a writer
Was not wanting to have her picture taken ever

A possible inversion of a yet deeper yearning
As the one revealed by Shakespeare in the Sonnets
For Beauty: first the despair at ever incarnating it in oneself
Second despairing of possessing it thru the Other, & finally
The sick & unassailable triumph of The Writer, the rare

Very rare one great enough to make a Beauty that won't die
Which if you think about it is something even God doesn't do
But the question of Beauty is no longer the question   not the question
I mean of our times   but it is   but we won't admit it   my stomach
Hurts from all the peanut butter I've eaten

You are allergic to peanuts and soy you are beautiful like a tuff & tall dove
There's a kind of truth most people are afraid of
Telling, which I understand because it would make them look bad
I am similarly afraid of telling such truths, but now I'm standing
Up on a crowded train I don't know that I'll be able to finish what I'm saying

Yes I will a man has just offered up his seat. Gentle city, today again
Underestimated by me! You looked so good on Google
Hangout this morning I know it sounds jejune
& though what we discussed about the subject FAKE
Apparently what they want you to teach at Parsons

Hurt me a little as it hurts me now how the man
What gave his seat up is now um adjusting something
In the pocket of his pants less than a foot from my face
In just such a way I really wish you were here
Already even though I don't yet know how to live

Part of me loathes poems the amorous ones
With a living addressee & feels as a reader
I not only have a right to but deserve an author's
Total devotion. I resent that other person behind their "you" want
My writers flayed & turning on the spit for my love or God's, that's it

And as for artists I don't know   in the fornicating wilderness
Through which we all have no choice but to move I don't think it wrong
To require of a thing at least passing devotion   the train
Vibrating everybody's genitals while half of us smash glass & spray machine
Gun bullets across our phones that shit used to badly unnerve me

I don't want to stop but it's time
For therapy. Therapy doesn't help very much. It helps
Exactly enough   sane slightly tantine presence
Bearing witness to all the normie things I never learned
Time management, the idea of not dying

Some things some beings
Just have more life in them fake as we all
May be, at least when we begin. And yes the future at times
Itself can seem the most pernicious form of fakery
You want to stay with the truth of having been destroyed

By what really did happen but now you must go on
I'm so full I can't really think, like
I just literally farted in a businessman's face but I had headphones
On so it was easy to ignore what I'd done. You've hit the road
Our laurel on your dashboard, you say, reminding you you will win

The moon was in Scorpio this AM, v moody &
Macho which we also were & this record's like a piece of carnival
Machinery, as they say, on crack. I read a beautiful essay
By Russell Brand about crack and dope and not smoking
Them. I hope "they" give him the credit he deserves

Soon if they have not yet. There are reasons a lapidary
Style's a better bet for a woman than say mine
Now I am peeing in REI. Now I'm in Whole Foods
Buying Pro Bars. Leopoldine gripped me by the hips
When she saw me. I really did

Eat a sick amount
Of peanut butter & after that mung
Beans simmered in New Mexican chilis etc
Cos that was all there was. Now I'm missing Women's
Gymnastics now I'm looking at progressive foods

I can see the money arpeggiating in transparent tubs
Of plantain chips (tostones) & Spicy Pub
Mix, snack foods of The People, bar fare of Joe and José
Six Pack, Fanfare for the Common Man
By Aaron Copland now gleaming on a shipping pallet

Ready to be turned into human money. I need chocolate
Almond milk and cold brew concentrate
If I'm going to clean the apartment and finish this
All in the same night and tell the boy
Named Offer I can't go to the Noguchi

With him cos I'm in love with you
Marin Marais comes into my ears
I'm thinking of Dolly Parton
Likening her heart to a bargain store, her butterfly
Tattoo and taking money from my little brother

I gave him Thurston & Eva's Necrobutcher book
The bent Peruvian man I met two days ago
In his new ice-cream shop full of toys
I still owe him a dollar. Except now it's tomorrow
I've paid him back with interest. This morning

I heard FINE AND MELLOW for the first time in an age
There are five lines a stanza in here open staves of slave
Wheat waving in oppressive ancient Egypt or if you prefer
The Americanizing trumpets of Aaron "studied counterpoint
With Boulanger" Copland, I don't know the things

It's right to care about, that's a feeling, my excesses go straight
Into my own pussy where I pay them not a penny
FINE AND MELLOW aches & aches with what is true
Your mouth the way you cock
Your head all over me   oblivion

Oblivion's the larger part   possibly
You know of my art, at least latterly
It has been. You never told me the meaning
Of the yellow pollen your grandmother blessed
Us with, so gently gently I looked it up online

Now you're texting me you've stopped in Soledad
For a sandwich so I ask you to please pour out
Some cola to the memory of Jonathan Jackson and George
Jackson   have you ever seen a string of shit hanging from a fish tank
Fish I asked you cos that was a little how I felt

Rather spiderish my poem unspooling out of me
Inside this imprisoned feeling. Men and women are not the same
Thanks for the pic of NATURE'S GIFT CHERRIES
"Remember here?" you asked & I do
I feel relaxed & amorous but at the edge

Of me's the sensation I'm being come into by six
Hundred years of colonial horror as in that Adrienne
Rich poem, the one that is for me her masterpiece
The archival impulse in dudes makes me impatient
But who, who is clean of it. & "dudes" made the place where we now meet

"Nothing, this foam" that's Mallarmé
In the poem called SALVATION or SALUTE or HELLO
Or HI. If I remember correctly he was an English
Teacher. Why don't people remember that when they come
All day all over what he left behind, taking him

So Oedipally seriously, "me already
On the poop," he writes I swear to God
Badly on purpose. White shit. Cream
Deth, the opposite of Prince. The day I earn
As much as Seth's the day he'll kiss my ass

At Leopoldine's reading she and the other female
Reader both treated twin subjects: impecunity
And getting stoned. Which will probably both be showing
Up a lot for a while as more young woman
Writers as they say EMERGE

Yesterday the director of the Belgian opera
Took me to lunch at the place I met Seth
Right off a redeye (I was) for breakfast
I drank two camparis & told him (Belgian opera man who by the way is Swiss)
My courtroom drama fantasy. It made me feel a little gross

& I don't see him going for it. Carina says she got called "an aggressive bitch"
At work today. I haven't read "The Painter
Of Modern Life" in half an age but I told Sheelagh
I'd translate "Correspondences" for the Symbolism
Show at the Frick.* Good job you have detected this is a New

York School of Poetry poem, for one thing, by the presence
Of the Frick with its Polish Rider so beloved of Frank O'Hara
And I'm going to show it to you when you get here
Even though you've already seen it but like the song
Says, I'll Take You There. My pen she glide so smoothly I can't

Stop.
        Actually I could stop and did but now I'm back again
Tex Ritter's singing RIDE RIDE RIDE. Seth had
An extremely Western shirt on when me met
The other week. A pregnant mare is not for riding
On. My hat's beside you as you drive you said. "A Step

Away From Them" is a poem I love. I can't remember
What happens in it right now though. "As I Walked Out
One Evening" is an Auden nonsense poem. A love
Poem I thought of as I walked out one morning into the porky
Air, families of Queens having slept in then all set in unison

To frying bacon. Now the cat is yowling
To the tune of RIDING INTO THE TOWN OF ALBUQUERQUE
Which is where I got that leather biker
Vest you like for $7. Where Byron would go on
And on a lady'd be wise to stop for my experience has shown me Romance

Looks better on the rich & lordly. SING COWBOY
SING goes the radio, not bidding Ariana go on, supremely cracker-
Ass & so hokey in its stylings you have to think it is "on purpose." Is my
    heart open
Like O'Hara says his poem is? I'm looking at his
Long-lost dick by Larry Rivers on SELECTED POEMS

Poets and painters, the joys of men, midcentury modernism
Whatever. My mean way of reducing to furniture all the old avant-
Gardes   I close my eyes and see your open
Hand, your fist. Chelsea just walked in. Hello I say
Her check has yet to come. Mine too. I guess I should go watch gymnastics

It's true what they say, that meaning can be made from anything. The real
Question might be must it & if so how. It's true what the Jews say
That the drawing-together of the two most disparate things is the real
Mark of intelligence. It's true what the Greeks say
That metaphor is transportation. And Art's

Demand that one turn a single idea into a thing, a place
A series, and do it elegantly, I've put that in my pipe
All over again and smoked it too. She picked
Her potted plant up off the floor but did not disturb
The dirt that it had left there. Transparency, surveillance

And whiteness. These are the three things. Compression
Dispersal, being everywhere at once, dark feelings, sustained attention
Paid to other people's major obsessions for minor & neglected modes
Of production, recent-past antiquing that can & must be turned to profit
The delicate art of sculpting as with a scalpel using the market as one
    among several tools

While all the while fleeing, seeming to flee from it or at least to appear
Relaxed. I'm a romantic & a voluptuary. I like
My food & my lord you. I like lying around & getting dressed
& walking around talking only to the shit-
Talking little Mozart of my mind

& I who was nowhere near Annandale-on-Hudson
How could I know SCORPION GRASS was another word for FORGET-
ME-NOT another blue flower
Of poetry not that I had read Novalis either
But I did see an early picture by Mondrian one time

Woke up with MOTOWN PHILLY in my head
Guess whose fault that is
I was gonna send you I LOVE YOUR SMILE by Shanice
But better you send my love to your grandmother
But I do love that song. Then all of a sudden the birds begin to scream

I'LL BUY YOU A CHEVROLET IF YOU LET ME DO
    SOMETHING TO YOU and
THE WAY YOU SHAKE THAT THING MAKES ME LOSE MY
    APPETITE
I had another dream I was in a cave filling out forms I couldn't
Understand. Then finally here
Came the warm jets, Crowley tears on my pillow...

2.

And he rode into town in his sores...
In the idiot cloth of a do-gooder...
Seated backwards upon an ass
Lo-res infinity in quiet carbonation about his head
Neither top nor bottom tier, plaintive strains on a kind of trombone...

Afternoon new music
The early dawn is very old, PRELUDE
TO THE AFTERNOON OF A FAUN except that wasn't it
At all, a daffodil or Wordsworth's sister
Dorothy, the poem Wm wrote to Toussaint Louverture

Worlds whipping themselves slowly into a cream
She left her broken beaded necklace scattered where it fell
"I'm paid a toll by every star inside this constellation"
Humid Alberti bass of allergens & other dander
Dusting haughtily the unchurned Milky Way

Moving unconsciously through this
Apparently open system... The color
Of neutrality, dignity's gender
The babysmooth cheek of specie
But I don't feel it's my job to resolve these things for you

& here's a little bag of preservatives inside a big bag
Of jerky & here are condom wrappers & fingernail parings
Engraved lead pipe fittings subtracted from the sites of their utility
Soft black lead scored with the long long names of demons
Held now in a white flame & now thrust deep in a cold mountain spring

Tears on my pillow... And what of the Dumpster™
Marked CENTURY WASTE, mess of tubes
Constituting the inspirational skyline of tomorrow?
Bay Bay it's fucking hot out
LADY U NEED A TABLE was the old sluggard's weird catcall

To me as I scrivened fast upon a legal pad outside the deli   & what if I did?
& who was he to say. Hélas, the human heart
Whose work can in no wise be avoided
The sluggard retreated indoors with a Family
Size bag of Lay's & quickly drew the curtains

My hair's at least as good as Seth's
Or Byron's so get down
On yr knees & pay me I mean pray
To the rainbow preserved in a jet
Of oil, the ordered entrails of a bird...

As I mounted the stair fat drops of acid
Rain bursted down upon me   I thought of Diego
With his sour and silky-looking hair
Diego who has fucked more women
Than you sir have even seen

The voice of Mick Jagger in Wild Horses
Always makes me think a little of cough syrup
But in a good way. I didn't come here
To resolve what you take to be MY DILEMMA
Though for there is sir NO DILEMMA

For love requires leisure, the love poem
Leisure too & slightly more. I have won
Myself both by my refusal
Ever to do anything else.
Next question?

Clear Channel, The Complete Poem
Brazilian Blowout by Ariana Reines
Moroccanoil Tome The First, too many Olympic
Rings on yr fingers my friend but we both know
That you are not my friend

What if it were true about the magic figures
As simple as writing them down
Roaring like a lion and never barring a seven
With a bar, just never crossing your legs? What if it is
As simple as that, and who can prove it isn't?

I am ready, frog titty, to receive the key
I am wearing my organdy windbreaker
I am shining like an alabaster
And painted pig
& I have hands & opposable thumbs

The pure religion of Blind Lemon Jefferson
The horrible deathlike stomachlike feeling
For I have read the stomach is the crypt of the body
And that death's deferral
Is another's upcycled trash. Now there are two fat men

Inside CENTURY WASTE & a truck goes by
With "TRAGEDY" tagged huge over the cab, quotation
Marks included. I was watching this woman eat a bag
Of Cool Ranch Doritos, it was ten in the morning & I swear
It said in the upper corner of her blue bag MADE WITH 100% DOG OIL

Tears on my pillow, silhouettes on the shade
Words like falling hairs upon repurposed sailcloth
Shipwrecks in the Cool Whip mind of Mallarmé pirates highwaymen
    knowing how to hit
The glancing edge of badness where the setting sun's acclaimed
By bolts of lightning falling fast into the hills

---

*ERRATUM: The 2017 exhibition *Delirium: The Art of the Symbolist Book*, for which
I translated "Correspondences" by Charles Baudelaire, was at the Morgan Library &
Museum, not the Frick.

MOSAIC

I wrote down what follows on or close to October 7, 2014. I wish I could be more precise about the date, but it isn't marked in my notebook. It is the transcript of the verbal portion of an encounter. It happened on a traffic island on Allen Street, facing Delancey, in New York City. The words aren't "mine."

I had just left rehearsal for MORTAL KOMBAT, a martial arts–inspired performance for the Whitney Museum that I created with the actor Jim Fletcher. Rehearsing this project was a physically exhausting and mentally fascinating adventure, involving punching and getting punched, slapping and getting slapped, dancing, tumbling, grappling, mirroring, and something we called "fake tai chi." The process opened strange and unusual currents in my body, and I often left rehearsal in a state of mildly euphoric mental numbness and physical elation.

Anyway, on this particular day, the sky was overcast and the weather mild as I made my way toward Delancey. I remember when the sun emerged from behind the clouds. It felt somehow warmer than usual. And something in me gave itself over to the pleasure of that warmth. I felt it entering me through the part of my head I sometimes call "my antenna," where my first white hairs grow, where my hair fell out while my mother was on Rikers Island, and where, when a truck drove into me near Léogâne, Haiti, in 2010, I developed a bump, though by all accounts I should have died.

The sun's warmth kept filling me, and what had begun as a slightly above-average warmth kept growing. It was starting to fill my body, and just before I totally surrendered to it, I had the inkling this might be something like the "bliss" I had heard about in old books. I had to sit down. There was even a bench to sit on right there, traffic streaming in both directions. I probably look like an idiot, I thought gently, if such a thought can be thought gently, and then I thought, I don't care.

Whatever bliss was, if this was it, it steadily gave way to rapture. I like the word rapture, *but the truth is no word exists for what I felt. It was love, of such ravishing totality that I don't know what to compare it to, and of such magnitude I could scarcely speak of it for two and a half years. I have never felt anything like it. That's not true. I have felt love, and this was love, but of a magnitude so enormous there was no way to undermine or deny it. There was no way to see around it and no desire for anything but to be filled with it. It was a feeling I cannot compare to anything. It was like what some poets have written about. It was like nothing any poet has ever been able to put into words. I know I'm failing right now. But I'm a human being, and you are, too, and perhaps you have felt something like this.*

I felt it filling me, and changing me, changing my cells, reorganizing me.

And then it began to speak. I was surprised and not surprised, and felt gently, lovingly taunted, mildly made fun of—the way I often do when something beyond me reminds me that I always knew it was there. This sensation of vague embarrassment—I'll come back to it—it's part of what made me trust the whole situation was "real," and it's part of the psychological mechanism of surrender for me. I notice the weird artifice of my personality, how clumsy it is, how it gets in the way of things, right before I drop it.

The sun began speaking, but not strictly to speak. Thoughtforms were being communicated to me whole, in a didactic and commanding voice that was not literally a voice, insofar as it wasn't audible to my ear. The voice had no sound, but it communicated its totality into me in a masculine tone—my entire body, my every cell, and every particle of my experience was being reorganized in order to shape and receive each thoughtform, each one delivered into me whole instant by instant, second by second, minute by minute.

Yes, the speaker was somehow a maleness but not in the sense of a human maleness; it had a personality and character to which it was bending and shaping what existed in my own brain and psyche and body, using my substance to communicate with and to me. The words that I wrote down are like one edge, one bevel, a single facet of a multidimensional communiqué, around which all details and nuances, all consequent thoughts and realities, spread in every direction of space and time.

When I remembered that I had my notebook in my bag, I fished it out and began transcribing. After I had been at it for a while, I realized I had my notebook upside down, that I was effectively writing right-to-left, like some parody of a Hebrew prophet. And there was something else. As I was fumbling for my notebook and pencil, I realized with some hilarity and considerable embarrassment that I was meeting my maker while wearing a beard. To be precise, I was wearing a zit beard. A beard made of acne. I had not put it on by choice.

I had been going through a difficult time. Aside from the demanding rehearsals for MORTAL KOMBAT, I had a prestigious new job where my direct superior was a tenured creep who liked to taunt me and other female colleagues and students with banter of a sexual nature, testing how much he could get away with before we'd balk, as if daring us to out ourselves as scolds and prudes if we mentioned we didn't much like his style of repartee; who quizzed his female students on their sex lives and stalked them on Facebook, who held bizarre ideas about the origin of breasts. ("Women evolved breasts so that men would look them in the eye while fucking them," he once declared to me, praising the research of his mentor...)

Although this creep was obviously a fool, and although I had withstood much worse than crass banter and "off-color" jokes at various jobs in my youth, the whole situation had caused a strange reaction in my body: old experiences, ones I had thought myself long done with, were suddenly filling me. As though my body were nothing but a garbage bag. The time I was raped, the time a boyfriend choked me in the subway, the time another boyfriend knocked me to the ground in front of my brother, the time a boyfriend spat in my face, and all these were "sensitive" men, gifted men, "feminist" men. These things and things like them, which I had thought myself done with, had latterly come back to fill me.

During the course of the one semester I did this job, I developed stage fright, which I had never had before. I would quake and tremble before readings, and at one fund-raiser reading for Black Lives Matter, my voice shook so much I thought I would burst into tears right there onstage. I delivered my poem on my knees, in a posture I hoped could pass for reverential but that I knew was nothing but cowering. But it wasn't just performing I was having trouble with. I had begun to doubt my capacities in language in general, and because I no longer felt I had the right to language, I had begun to doubt my right to live. Had the "freedom" and the sexuality in my work made my boss feel he had the right to belittle me so casually, to bring sexual talk into spaces where it really did not need to be? I had begun to go silent. I could feel it happening to me, as though concrete were filling my cells. The more silent I grew, the more silence I wanted. Silence had become almost voluptuous—it was becoming my place of refuge. It became indistinguishable from rage. I tended this silence/rage in the darkness of my organs. I called it my privacy.

What I am trying to explain to you is how I grew my beard. My cheeks and chin had sprouted painful sores, like the sores King David or someone complains of in the Psalms. Of course, Job too, and other biblical figures, suffered boils. At the time, I referred to my beard only inwardly—I liked to mock myself about "the serrated gates of my face."

Shame had made me grow a beard, the kind of beard that I was in a position to grow, and shame is what festering silence, what repressed rage turns into. *Of course my beard also* caused *me shame, in the recursive and exponential math of spiritual truths. I had Jew's horns. Witch tits. I was afflicted with the kind of blemishes that might have gotten me killed in medieval Europe or seventeenth-century Salem. I would occasionally try to remind myself that my inner torment had put me—facial hair–wise—in line with the rabbis and sages, the elders, Fathers Time, pharaohs, the bureaucrats disguised as holy men, and the real holy men of the ages, but the thought that the wages of my suffering might for ancient men have meant a badge of wisdom or authority only made it easier to deride my sorry lot in the now. And while being forced to live my life out in the open with a face so afflicted was obviously a torture (it also physically hurt), this particular colloquy—which I privately came to call MOSAIC—and this too was a joke, since like Moses I was afflicted with a [temporary] speech impediment—this event was probably the only encounter for which such a beard could be the ideal and really the only possible garment for my naked woman's face.*

The first time I spoke publicly about MOSAIC was in a keynote lecture at OCCULT POETICS, a conference at Concordia University in Montreal, in February 2017.

REALITY IS PERCEPTIBLE

SITUATIONS ARE CELLS

PEOPLE DON'T KNOW HOW
TO USE THEIR TALENTS

ANALOGY IS THE STRUCTURING
PRINCIPLE OF THE UNIVERSE

THE SUFFERING OF WOMAN IS THE
TRUE STORY OF THE UNIVERSE

WE HAVE TO UNDERSTAND OURSELVES AT ALL COSTS

NATURE EXTENDS FROM US

NATURE MIRRORS US

WATER→MIRROR
\   /
WINDOW

EACH PEOPLE HAS THE GIFT OF ITS CATASTROPHE

LEARN HOW TO USE THIS GIFT OR MEET YOUR PERIL

EARTH IS SPECIAL

PEOPLE FROM ALL OVER THE UNIVERSE
WILL COME HERE

THERE IS NO "BACK" TO GET TO

"GOD" DIDN'T DIE

HE'S JUST NOT THE ONLY GOD IN THE UNIVERSE

THE MOON IS SUPERIOR TO THE SUN INSOFAR AS SHE
HAS HAD THE NIGHT TO KNOW HE IS NOT
THE ONLY GOD IN THE UNIVERSE

DIFFERENCE IS MEANT TO BE COMEDY

DIFFERENCE IS A TOY

NAZISM WAS AN INVITATION TO THE WORLD TO
RECKON WITH THE NATURE OF EVIL

EACH THING TEACHES

WHEN FACED WITH EVIL

LEARN ITS SECRET

WHAT URGENT DISEASE

DEFICIENCY WITHIN MY OWN SOUL

DOES THIS WRETCHED SYMPTOM SIGNIFY

WE DO NEED EVERY KIND OF STORY

BECAUSE THERE IS EVERY KIND OF PERSON

YET STILL, GREAT ART IS CRUCIAL

FOR THE WORLD TO WATCH, WHEN IT WATCHES,
DIVINITY IN SPLENDOR

RATHER THAN WHAT WE'RE WATCHING NOW,
WHILE LEARNING TO WATCH

THE WORLD ALWAYS SUSTAINS THE MAXIMUM
SUFFERING IT CAN BEAR, ACCORDING TO
THE NATURE OF ITS AGE

THERE WILL ALWAYS BE THE MAXIMUM
POSSIBLE DESTRUCTION IN A GIVEN TIME

THIS IS WHY THE OTHER WORLD
HAS ALWAYS NEEDED TO BE CREATED

KNOWING THAT THE WORLD HAS ALWAYS SUSTAINED
AND WILL ALWAYS SUSTAIN THE MAXIMUM
OF DESTRUCTION POSSIBLE

IS WHY THE OTHER WORLD HAS ALWAYS
AND WILL ALWAYS NEED TO BE CREATED

EVERYONE HAS A STAR

THIS IS WHY WE
PRACTICE DIALOGUE

WE'RE LEARNING

OUR SOLAR SYSTEM IS ANALOGOUS TO THE UNIVERSE

THE DEEPER INTO THE CELL WE GET

THE MORE KINDS OF PEOPLE WE PRODUCE

THE MORE WE LEARN ABOUT THE CELL

THE MORE WE HAVE TO KNOW ABOUT THE PEOPLE

MERCURY ALSO TEACHES

"I WANT TO BE LIKE"

AND THE RISKS THAT GO WITH "I WANT TO BE LIKE"

TO TEACH US ABOUT THE PRINCIPLE OF
LIKENESS THAT GOVERNS THE UNIVERSE

IT'S TRUE THAT THE OLDER
A THING IS THE BETTER IT IS

EXCEPT WITH FOOD & FOODLIKE PRINCIPLES

NOT THE SOCK ON YOUR FOOT

BUT ANY SPECK OF MATTER IN RELATION

TO THE DIGNITY OF AGE THAT IS THE WINERY

MERCURY FAVORS WOMEN

AND CHILDREN

BECAUSE WE KNOW WHAT IT'S LIKE

TO LONG TO BE EVERYTHING

TO LEARN BY IMITATION

TO LISTEN

I GAVE YOU NO MAN FOR A FATHER

NO MAN COULD STAND BETWEEN ME AND YOU

MEDICINE IS DIVINE

NOT AS IT IS SHOWN

BUT AS IT SHOULD BE

DIVINE SCIENCE

DIVINE SCIENTIST

MEDICINE WOULD BE DIVINE

THE REASON GREAT ART MATTERS IS

SEE AS I SEE

WHATEVER YOU HAVE BEEN WATCHING
SHOULD HAVE TAUGHT YOU BY NOW

THE TIME OF SPECTACLE WILL PASS

TECHNOLOGY IS FOR COMMUNICATION

TECHNOLOGY EVOLVED SOLELY FOR THE
PURPOSE OF DIVINE COMMUNICATION

ALL ITS OTHER FORMS ARE BYPRODUCTS

THERE IS NOTHING A PERSON CANNOT LOVE

EVERYTHING HAS A NATURE

FIND OUT YOURS

ACKNOWLEDGMENTS

For day and night thy hand was heavy upon me: my moisture is turned into the drought of summer.—Psalms

To the many friends who have opened your homes to this project and shared your lives with me, thank you. This book is for you.

Grateful acknowledgment to Fence, Semiotext(e), The MacDowell Colony, the Lucas Artists Residency Program at Montalvo, the University of East Anglia, the T. S. Eliot House, and the Dora Maar House for their hospitality, and to the many institutions large and small that have hosted live events, teaching, and performances. Thank you also to the Quba Siltan Êzîd in Tbilisi, to my students and astrology clients, and to my visionary teachers and colleagues. I bow to you.

"A PARTIAL HISTORY" – *Poetry Magazine* (2019)

"ARENA" – *Spike* (2019)

"TWELFTH NIGHT" – *Beyond Relief: Two Writers' Work & Words* by Celina Su and Ariana Reines, Belladonna* Material Lives Chaplet Series #151 (2013); *The Prelude* (2015)

"DREAM HOUSE" – Commissioned by Ruba Katrib for the group exhibition *Better Homes* at SculptureCenter, Long Island City, NY (2013); *Boston Review* (2013)

"SANDRA" – www.arianareines.tumblr.com (July 22, 2015)

"RAMAYANA" – Commissioned by Paul B. Preciado for the exhibition *The Passion According to Carol Rama, MACBA* Barcelona (2014), *FENCE* (2019)

"SOMETHING INSIDE ME" – Commissioned by Nicole Eisenman for *Parkett* (2012)

"A VALEDICTION FORBIDDING MOURNING" – Artforum.com (2018)

"DISTINGUISHED $ENTIMENTS" – Commissioned by Friedrich Kunath for *I Don't Worry Anymore*, Rizzoli (2018)

"RUNNING NYMPH" – *Harper's Magazine* (2019)

"WHO HERE UNDERSTANDS ENGLISH" – *The New Republic* (2018), *Animal Shelter* (2018)

"BEAUTY" – *Poem-a-Day* (2017)

"SKULL&BONES" – *BOMB Magazine* (2017)

"IN BLOOM" – *New York Tyrant* (2017)

"TRY NOT TO DISTURB THE WILD PALMS," "CÉLEUR" – *Pioneer Works* (2017)

"WASTING AWAY IN THIS VANILLA DARKNESS" – *Lit Hub* (2017), *FENCE* (2019)

"QUEENS," "REPORT" – *FENCE* (2019)

"THURSDAY" (full section) – Chapbook by Spork Press (2013); *SPELLS: 21st Century Occult Poetry*, edited by Sarah Shin and Rebecca Tamás (2018)

"THE SADDEST YEAR OF MY LIFE" – *Lenny* (2015)

"HEGELING BEFORE THE GLASS" – *Lit Hub* (2017)

"WELLFLEET" – *Adult Magazine* (2013)

"TIFFANY'S POEMS" (full section) – Chapbook by The Song Cave (2014)

"THE LONG LOVE THAT IN MY THOUGHT DOTH HARBOR" – *February* (2015)

"NINE MOONS" – Commissioned by Yana Toyber for *This Time* (2015)

"NINE NEOCLASSICAL POEMS" (full section) – Written for and originally presented in PUBIC SPACE, a sculpture collaboration with Oscar Tuazon at Stuart Shave / Modern Art, London (2016)

"CRYSTAL GEYSER" – Signed and numbered limited edition broadside produced by Richard Hell for his curated series at Symphony Space, NY (2015)

"THE WAR ON APRIL" – *The Claudius App* (2013)

"FKN ZIGGURATS," "IT IS A SUCKLING LOVE," "DEMOCRACY NOW," "RAPES EONS FISHERIES," "YOUR POEM," "I CAN'T EAT YOU CAN'T SLEEP," and "WHO AREN'T WE" – *Boston Review* (2017)

"PILGRIMS' PROGRESS" – Commissioned by Susan Martin for the exhibition *Love Among the Ruins* at Howl Happening, NY (2017), *The Believer Logger* (2017), Animal Shelter (2018)

"OPEN FIFTHS" – Commissioned by Seth Price for the exhibition SOCIAL SYNTHETIC, Stedelijk Museum, Amsterdam, Holland (2017)